W9-CTQ-438

weber

GRILL OUT!

Pictured on the cover: *Marinated Mixed Grill* (see recipe, page 51) and *Grilled Vegetables* (see tip, page 131).

This seal assures you that every recipe appearing in *Grill Out!* has been tested in the Better Homes and Gardens® Test Kitchen. This means that each recipe is practical and reliable, and meets high standards of taste appeal.

Produced by Meredith Publishing Services, Locust at 17th Street, Des Moines, IA 50336.

GRILL OUT!

Ahh—the great taste of barbecue! There's nothing like it. When you try the delicious recipes from our special collection, you'll find plenty of reasons to fire up your Weber® charcoal or gas grill. That's because there are over 200 outstanding recipes and ideas to choose from. And there's so much variety, you can cook your entire meal on the grill. Start by selecting an entrée from the Meat, Poultry, or Fish and Seafood section. Then turn to the Exciting Extras section for an appetizer, vegetable, bread, or dessert to grill with the entrée.

By referring to the recipes, general barbecuing information, helpful tips, and handy grilling charts in *Grill Out!*, you'll get superb results every time you fire up your Weber grill. You'll discover some of the best barbecuing recipes and techniques developed by Weber over almost four decades of experience in the barbecue business. And to ensure your grilling success, we've tested every recipe in the Better Homes and Gardens® Test Kitchen.

Almost anything can be prepared on the grill. Once a few barbecue basics are mastered, beginners as well as experienced cooks can turn out memory-making outdoor meals to fit any occasion, from a simple family dinner to a gala special occasion.

We think you'll agree that barbecuing is the perfect way to entertain. Turn to the International menus, and you can treat guests to a taste of France, Germany, New Zealand, Italy, China, Scandinavia, or the Caribbean Islands. Each menu includes an easy-to-follow timetable to help you simplify planning and preparation. Once you've tried one menu, you'll want to try them all.

Enjoy—and happy barbecuing!

TABLE OF CONTENTS

Next time you're expecting a crowd, fire up the grill for *Barbecued Beef Brisket*. While the brisket grills on its own, set up the sandwich buffet (see recipe, page 30).

4

BARBECUING BASICS

CHARCOAL GRILLING MADE EASY

DIRECT METHOD

This method is best for foods that grill in less than 25 minutes or for flat foods such as burgers, steaks, chops, and boneless chicken breasts. Turn these foods once halfway through grilling time.

Open all vents before starting the fire. Spread charcoal briquettes in a single layer on the lower (charcoal) grill, then push into a pyramid-shaped pile and ignite. When the briquettes have a light coating of gray ash, use long-handled tongs to spread them again in a single layer for grilling.

Put the cooking grill in place, then place the food on the cooking grill. Cover the grill, leaving all vents open, and grill food as directed in recipe.

See instructions for grilling kabobs on page 14.

FIRE UP!

A great barbecue begins with a good fire. First, make sure the vents on the top and bottom of your Weber® charcoal grill are completely open.

Arrange the charcoal briquettes for Direct grilling (see right) or Indirect grilling (see page 7). Light the briquettes 25 to 30 minutes before you begin cooking. (Leave lid off kettle while the briquettes are starting.) A light coat of gray ash on the briquettes indicates that the fire is ready.

FAST FIRE STARTERS

If you're using untreated charcoal briquettes, choose one of these starters to light your fire successfully.

• *Liquid or jellied starter:* Let starter soak into the briquettes for a few minutes, then light in several places.

• *Solid starter:* Place two or three starters on the lower (charcoal) grill, then light with a match. Pile the briquettes on top of the burning starter cubes.

• *Electric starter:* Put some briquettes on the lower (charcoal) grill, place the starter on top, then pile more briquettes over the starter. Turn on the starter for 10 to 12 minutes.

• *Chimney starter:* Stuff a crumpled sheet of newspaper into the bottom of the chimney. Place on the lower (charcoal) grill, pour briquettes into the chimney, and ignite the paper.

INDIRECT METHOD

This method is best for foods that would normally be roasted or that require more than 25 minutes grilling time, such as hams, meat loaves, ribs, roasts, turkeys, and whole fish.

Open all vents before starting the fire. Position charcoal rails as near the outside edge on the lower (charcoal) grill as possible. This allows a large area in the center for the drip pan. Place an equal number of charcoal briquettes on the left and right sides. (See chart on bottom right for the correct number to use.)

Ignite the briquettes. Let them burn 25 to 30 minutes or till they have a light coating of gray ash. For even heat, be sure the briquettes are burning evenly on each side. If one side is hotter than the other side, use long-handled tongs to rearrange briquettes.

Center a drip pan on the lower charcoal grill. Then insert the cooking grill with the handles positioned directly over the briquettes so additional briquettes can be added through the openings by the handles. Place the food in center

of the cooking grill directly above the drip pan. Cover the grill, leaving all vents open, and grill food as directed in recipe.

Indirect grilling is a no-peek cooking method. In fact, every time you uncover the grill you let heat escape and add as much as 15 minutes to the grilling time. Let foods grill the minimum time given in the recipe before checking for doneness. Because heat circulates around the foods much like in a convection oven, you do not need to turn the foods.

DIRECT METHOD	**INDIRECT METHOD**

INDIRECT METHOD How Many Charcoal Briquettes to Use		
Diameter of grill (inches)	Number briquettes needed on each side for the first hour	Number briquettes to add to each side every hour
26¾	30	9
22½	25	8
18½	16	5

GAS GRILLING MADE EASY

SIMPLE START-UP

With gas grilling, start-up is as easy as turning on a burner on your range.

To start your Weber® Genesis® Gas Barbecue, open the lid. Check that all burner control knobs are turned to OFF and that the fuel scale reads more than "E." Next turn the gas on at the source.

Light with the igniter switch or a match if necessary, according to the manufacturer's directions. Check through the viewing port in front to be sure the burner is lit.

Close the lid and preheat the grill to 500°–550°F (260°–288°C). This will take 10 to 15 minutes. Then adjust the heat controls as the recipe directs.

DIRECT METHOD

When using your gas grill for the recipes in this book, you'll use the Direct Method only for preheating and searing steaks; grilling is completed by the Indirect Method. Grill all other foods entirely by the Indirect Method.

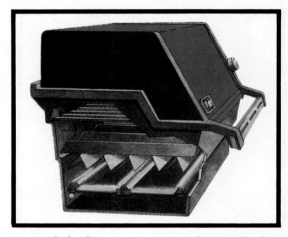

Searing helps keep meat moist and juicy. The hot fat that drips from the meat creates the smoke that gives foods a distinctive barbecued flavor.

To sear well-trimmed steaks, turn all burners to HIGH. Preheat grill to 500°–550°F (260°–288°C) with the lid down. Place the meat on the preheated cooking grill. Close lid and sear first side of steaks over High Heat, allowing 2 minutes for 1-inch-thick steaks and 4 minutes for 1½- and 2-inch-thick steaks. Then turn steaks and grill Indirect over Medium Heat, turning once halfway through grilling time. (See chart on page 15 for steak timings.)

If excess flaring occurs during searing, turn the center burner to OFF till the flaring subsides. Then turn the center burner to MEDIUM or LOW to complete searing.

DIRECT METHOD

INDIRECT METHOD

Use this method to complete grilling steaks after searing and for grilling roasts, whole or cut-up poultry, whole fish, fish steaks and fillets, vegetables, breads, and desserts.

Preheating the grill before grilling is important. Preheat grill to 500°–550°F (260°–288°C) with the lid down. Place food in center of the cooking grill with the front and back burners set at MEDIUM and the center burner turned to OFF (MEDIUM-OFF-MEDIUM, indicated in chart at right as MOM). With the lid closed and the center burner turned to OFF, the Genesis Gas Barbecue cooks much like a convection oven. The heat circulates inside the grill, so turning the food is not necessary. All preheating and cooking is done with the lid down. No peeking—heat is lost every time you lift the lid.

GAS GRILLING CHARTS

Each recipe in this book includes the grilling method and heat setting to use on your gas grill. The charts below will help you determine the correct burner setting once you've preheated the grill. For example, if the recipe directions say to grill Indirect over Medium Heat and you own a three-burner gas grill, such as the Weber Genesis Gas Barbecue, you would turn the front burner to MEDIUM, the center burner to OFF, and the back burner to MEDIUM (MOM) and grill according to the timings given in the recipe. If you own a two-burner gas grill, such as the Weber Genesis Junior Gas Barbecue, simply turn the front and back burners to MEDIUM (M-M) and grill according to the timings given in the recipe.

INDIRECT METHOD
Three-Burner Weber Genesis Gas Barbecues

Heat	Setting	Front Burner	Center Burner	Back Burner
Low	LOL	Low	Off	Low
Medium	MOM	Medium	Off	Medium
High	HOH	High	Off	High

INDIRECT METHOD
Two-Burner Weber Genesis Junior Gas Barbecue

Heat	Setting	Front Burner	Back Burner
Low	LL	Low	Low
Medium	MM	Medium	Medium
High	HH	High	High

INDIRECT METHOD

GEAR UP WITH WEBER® ACCESSORIES

WEBER GRILL WORKS™ ACCESSORY

This multipurpose barbecue accessory has a porcelain-enameled steel base and extra-heavy nickel-plated steel accessory pieces that stand up to years of barbecuing. Use it as a rack for ribs, chops, or chicken pieces. Or, use it as a sturdy drip pan holder.

HELPFUL TOOLS

For safety's sake, always use long-handled tools when grilling. Basic necessities are a turner, basting brush, fork, and tongs. Weber offers a variety of high-quality tools and other accessories for successful grilling.

Or, convert it in seconds to a roast holder that can hold a large drip pan for roasting and carrying the cooked roast.

Or, add skewers and it becomes a shish kabob rack. The attachments snap in and out for easy cleanup.

CORN 'N' TATER™ HOLDERS

These nickel-plated steel holders sit directly on the cooking grill to save space. The metal prongs speed vegetable cooking, too. The two-prong holders come four per pack.

FOIL PANS

For easy cleanup, Weber 8x5¼-inch heavy-gauge aluminum pans line the Genesis® Gas Barbecue grease catch pan. Or, use them as handy disposable cooking pans for grilling meats, vegetables, and fruits. The 13x9-inch size make perfect drip pans for the Indirect method of grilling. Both sizes come in packages of 10.

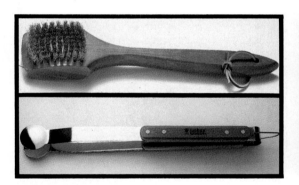

GRILL BRUSH

A rustproof brass-bristled grill brush quickly removes food residue from the cooking grill.

WEBERGRABBERS® TONGS

WeberGrabbers Tongs have long, hardwood handles for a safe, sure grip. Use this handy tool to turn foods without piercing or for moving charcoal briquettes.

WEBER THERMOMETER

This instant-read thermometer gives accurate internal food temperatures so you'll know when barbecued foods are cooked to perfection. See page 12 for tips on using the thermometer.

If you are unable to find the Weber grill accessories shown here at your local Weber dealer, call 800/446-1071 or 708/705-8660. Or, write to Weber-Stephen Products Co., Customer Service Center, 560 Hicks Road, Palatine, IL 60067 for an order blank.

ADDITIONAL GRILLING TIPS

USING A THERMOMETER

The handy Weber® Dual-Purpose Thermometer is an instant-read thermometer. It lets you keep tabs on the cooking temperature inside the grill. Or, you can use the probe to check the doneness of food. Replace the thermometer in the lid when not in use. Never leave it in the meat while grilling.

Always use a barbecue mitt to protect your hands when removing the Dual-Purpose Thermometer from the grill to check the internal temperature of food. For foods, such as roasts or whole turkeys, where directions say to insert the thermometer into the meat before grilling, be sure to use an oven-safe thermometer to monitor the internal temperature.

For steaks and chops, insert the probe of the Dual-Purpose Thermometer through the side of the meat so the tip is in the center of the meat. To check a roast, insert the probe so the tip is in the center of the meat, and not touching fat or bone. Allow a few seconds for the temperature to register.

Remove roasts from the grill when the internal temperature registers five degrees less than the desired doneness and let stand 10 to 15 minutes before carving. During the standing time the meat continues to cook and will be easier to slice.

ROTISSERIE COOKING

The slow, steady turning of a rotisserie makes meat or poultry baste itself. For best results, the food must be balanced on the spit. Insert the spit rod lengthwise through the center of the meat or poultry and secure with the holding forks.

Test the balance by holding the ends of the rod in the palms of your hands and rotating the rod gently. If the meat flops or turns unevenly, readjust the holding forks or the spit rod and retest the balance. The Weber Heavy-Duty Rotisserie has a counter-balancing device to grill food evenly every time.

SMOKE COOKING

Where there's smoke, there's flavor! You can smoke-cook in any covered grill or a smoker.

Hickory and oak add robust taste; mesquite gives a light smoked flavor. All are good with beef, pork, poultry, and salmon. Fruitwoods such as apple and cherry have more delicate flavors and complement poultry well. Alder has a delicate aroma and is especially good with fish. Softwoods, such as evergreen or maple, are not recommended for smoking because their resins discolor foods and give a bitter taste.

Once you're familiar with wood flavors, sample grapevine cuttings, orange peel, garlic, parsley, basil, or dried fennel stalks. Wet these materials before adding to hot charcoal briquettes.

Smoking woods are available as chips or chunks. Chips are ideal for foods cooked by the Direct Method. One or two handfuls of wet wood chips placed on top of the hot briquettes will satisfy most tastes. Chunks burn longer than chips and are perfect for foods with longer cooking times. Wood chunks can be used as the sole source of cooking fuel or act in combination with charcoal.

When adding wood to a burning charcoal fire, be sure to soak chunks in water at least one hour before grilling; chips at least 30 minutes. This causes them to smolder rather than flame when you add them to the hot briquettes. Always cover the grill while grilling so the aroma of the smoking wood has a chance to fully penetrate the food. When the wood starts smoking, begin grilling. The more chips or chunks you use, the more powerful the flavor. Use less wood for more subtle flavor.

Smoke-cooked food may still look a little pink when fully cooked. To be sure of doneness, check the internal temperature with a meat thermometer.

Smoke-cooking adds flavor to food but doesn't preserve it. Eat smoked foods while they're hot, and refrigerate leftovers promptly.

HELPFUL HINTS FOR A BETTER BARBECUE

Store charcoal in a dry place. Otherwise it will absorb moisture and won't burn well. If you store charcoal outdoors, keep it in a weatherproof container with a tight lid.

Tilt the lid of a charcoal grill as you remove it. If you lift the lid off straight up, ashes will fly onto the food or into the drip pan.

Want to heat a sauce on the grill? Be sure to use a saucepan with a heatproof handle. Or heat sauce in a Weber 8x5¼-inch aluminum pan.

Trim excess fat from steaks and roasts, leaving no more than a scant ¼ inch of fat. This makes the meat easier to grill and healthier to eat!

Always use tongs for turning meat. Then you'll avoid piercing the meat, which causes it to lose its natural juices.

A timer is an invaluable aid for barbecue cooks. Set it to remind you to check the food on the grill while you prepare the rest of the meal.

The front of your charcoal grill should face the wind to provide the best air flow for the fire.

SAFETY ALWAYS

All manufacturers of charcoal and gas grills have specific instruction manuals and warnings as to proper use. Please follow these instructions and pay close attention to the warnings as failure to do so can result in damage to property and serious personal injury or death.

Always keep children and pets a safe distance from a hot grill.

Never use a charcoal or gas grill indoors or in a closed garage or enclosed patio; they are outdoor cooking appliances.

Never use gasoline or other highly volatile fluids as starter; they may explode. Never add liquid starter to hot—or even warm—coals.

To reduce the chance of an accidental fire, place your grill on a nonflammable surface and away from wooden railings, trees, and bushes. Be sure the grill stands level.

CLEANING THE GRILL

To make cleanup easier, take a preventive step by spraying the cooking grill with nonstick spray coating before adding the food.

After each use, loosen residue on the cooking grill of your charcoal grill with a brass-bristled grill brush or crumpled aluminum foil. Then wipe with paper towels. Remove accumulated ashes frequently.

Clean a charcoal barbecue thoroughly once a year. Remove the ashes; remove the cooking and charcoal grills. Spray porcelain surfaces with oven cleaner, let stand, and wipe out with paper towels. Wash with a mild detergent and water. Rinse and wipe dry.

To clean your gas grill easily, place a large piece of heavy-duty aluminum foil, shiny side down, on top of the cooking grill. Leave the gaps on the sides of the cooking grid open. Ignite the grill and turn all burners to HIGH. Close the hood and let the grill heat 10 to 15 minutes, then turn all burners to OFF. Let grill cool. Wipe off grease inside the lid with paper towels. Crumple the foil and use to brush ash and burned food particles from the cooking grid and Flavorizer® Bars. Remove and brush out bottom tray. Wash the tray and grease catch pan in hot soapy water. Rinse with clear water and dry.

KABOBS MADE EASY!

Add some fun to your next outdoor barbecue. Bring out an assortment of meats, vegetables, fruits, and sauces, then invite guests to assemble their own kabobs.

PREPARING KABOBS
Prepare meat and vegetables as directed. Prepare sauce as directed. On skewers alternately thread ingredients, leaving space between pieces to ensure even grilling.

GRILLING KABOBS:
Prepare grill as directed below. Place kabobs on the cooking grill. Grill 10 to 12 minutes or till meat, vegetables, and/or fruit are tender, turning once and brushing with sauce halfway through grilling time.

• **Charcoal:** When preparing the fire for kabobs, use about *three-fourths* the amount of charcoal briquettes that you would normally use for grilling Direct. One layer of sparsely arranged briquettes provides the right heat.

• **Gas:** Close the grill and preheat to 500°-550°F (260°-288°C). Grill kabobs Indirect over Medium Heat.

Always wear barbecue mitts to protect your hands while turning kabobs—metal skewers become intensely hot.

If using wood skewers—soak them in water for at least 1 hour before using so they don't burn.

MEAT
Allow 4 servings per pound of meat or fish (3 servings per pound of shrimp with shell or chicken with the bone).

Beef sirloin, boneless: Cut into 1-inch pieces.

Pork, lean boneless: Cut into 1-inch pieces.

Sausage, fully cooked: Cut into 2-inch pieces.

Lamb, boneless: Cut into 1-inch pieces.

Chicken breasts: Skin, bone, and cut into 1-inch pieces.

Fish: Choose from tuna, swordfish, shark, catfish, seabass steaks or fillets. Thaw, if frozen. Cut into 1-inch pieces.

Shrimp: Thaw, if frozen. Shell and devein shrimp.

Sea Scallops: Thaw, if frozen.

VEGETABLES
Artichoke hearts, frozen: Thaw.

Broccoli or cauliflower flowerets: Precook 1 to 2 minutes.

Carrots, baby: Precook 4 to 5 minutes.

Corn, fresh ears: Cut into 1-inch pieces. Precook 6 to 8 minutes.

Green onion: Cut into 1-inch pieces.

Jicama: Peel and cut into 1-inch pieces.

Leeks: Cut into 1-inch pieces. Precook 4 to 5 minutes.

Mushrooms, large: Precook 1 to 2 minutes.

Onion wedges: Precook 4 to 5 minutes.

Pepper, sweet red or green: Cut into 1-inch pieces.

Potatoes, whole tiny new: Halve potatoes. Precook 12 to 15 minutes.

Summer squash: Cut into ½-inch slices. Precook 1 to 2 minutes.

Tomatoes, cherry or wedges: Add to skewers during last minute of grilling.

FRUITS
Apple wedges
Orange slices
Papaya: Peel, seed, and cut into 1-inch pieces.

Pineapple, fresh: Cut into 1-inch pieces.

SAUCES
Refer to pages 110–113 for sauces to compliment your kabobs.

STEAKS

Place steaks on the cooking grill.

Charcoal: Direct (pages 6-7)

Grill steaks for the time given in the chart or till desired doneness, turning once halfway through grilling time.

Gas: Sear Direct/High Heat (pages 8-9)
Grill Indirect/Medium Heat (pages 8-9)

For searing, allow 2 minutes for 1-inch-thick steaks and 4 minutes for 1½- and 2-inch-thick steaks. Turn steaks and finish grilling Indirect over Medium heat, turning once halfway through remaining grilling time. The cooking times in the chart include searing, explained on page 8.

CUT	THICKNESS/ WEIGHT	APPROXIMATE COOKING TIME RARE 140°F (60°C)	MEDIUM 160°F (71°C)	WELL-DONE 170°F (77°C)
Flank steak	1–1½ lbs	10–15 min	15–19 min	—
New York strip	1 in.	8–10 min	10–12 min	12–14 min
Ribeye	¾ in.	5–7 min	7–9 min	9–11 min
Steaks	1 in.	6–7 min	7–9 min	9–11 min
Porterhouse, rib, ribeye, sirloin, T-Bone, tenderloin, and top loin	1½ in.	10–12 min	12–15 min	15–19 min
	2 in.	15–17 min	17–19 min	19–22 min

ROASTS

Insert a meat thermometer into the meat. Place meat, fat side up, in center of cooking grill. Grill Indirect for time given in chart or till thermometer registers desired internal temperature.

Charcoal: Indirect (pages 6-7)
Gas: Indirect/Medium Heat (pages 8-9)

CUT	WEIGHT	APPROXIMATE COOKING TIME RARE 140°F (60°C)	MEDIUM 160°F (71°C)	WELL-DONE 170°F (77°C)
*Brisket, fresh	5–6 lbs	—	2½–3 hrs	—
Eye of round roast	2–3 lbs	50 min–1¼ hrs	1¼–1¾ hrs	1¾–2 hrs
Rib eye roast	4–6 lbs	1–1½ hrs	1½–2 hrs	2–2½ hrs
Rib roast, small end	4–6 lbs	1¼–2¼ hrs	2¼–2¾ hrs	2¾–3¼ hrs
Sirloin roast, boneless	4–6 lbs	1½–2 hrs	2–2½ hrs	2½–3 hrs
Tenderloin roast				
Half	2–3 lbs	45–60 min	—	—
Whole	4–5 lbs	50 min–1½ hrs	—	—
Tip roast	3–5 lbs	1–1¾ hrs	1¾–2¼ hrs	2¼–2¾ hrs
	6–8 lbs	1¾–2½ hrs	2½–3 hrs	3–3½ hrs
Top round roast	4–6 lbs	1¼–1¾ hrs	1¾–2¼ hrs	2–2½ hrs

*See Barbecued Beef Brisket recipe on page 30 for special slow-cooking instructions.

CHOPS AND STEAKS

Place chops on cooking grill. Grill for the time given in the chart or till desired doneness, turning once halfway through grilling time.

Charcoal: Grill steaks and ½- to ¾-inch-thick chops **Direct**. Grill thicker chops **Indirect**. **(See pages 6-7.)**
Gas: Indirect/Medium Heat (pages 8-9)

CUT	THICKNESS	APPROXIMATE COOKING TIME MEDIUM 160°F (71°C)	WELL-DONE 170°F (77°C)
Blade steak	½ in.	10–12 min	12–14 min
Chops			
Loin, rib,	¾ in.	12–14 min	14–19 min
and shoulder	1¼–1½ in.	35–40 min	40–45 min

ROASTS

Insert a meat thermometer into the meat. Place the meat, fat side up, in center of the cooking grill. Grill Indirect for the time given in the chart or till thermometer registers the desired internal temperature.

Charcoal: Indirect (pages 6-7)
Gas: Indirect/Medium Heat (pages 8-9)

CUT	THICKNESS/ WEIGHT	APPROXIMATE COOKING TIME 140°F (60°C)	MEDIUM 160°F (71°C)	WELL-DONE 170°F (77°C)
Ham, fully cooked				
Slice	1 in.	12 min	—	—
Boneless portion	3–4 lbs	50 min–1 hr	—	—
	4–6 lbs	1–2 hrs	—	—
Smoked picnic	5–8 lbs	1–2½ hrs	—	—
Whole ham, bone in	10–12 lbs	2–2¾ hrs	—	—
Loin blade or sirloin roast	3–4 lbs	—	1–2 hrs	2–3 hrs
Loin center rib roast, backbone loosened	3–5 lbs	—	1–2 hrs	2–2½ hrs
Rib crown roast	4–6 lbs	—	1¾–2 hrs	2–3 hrs
Ribs				
Country-style ribs	3–4 lbs	—	—	1¼–1½ hrs
Loin back ribs or spareribs	3–4 lbs	—	—	1–1½ hrs
Tenderloin	¾–1 lb	—	25–35 min	30–45 min
Top loin roast, boneless				
Single loin	2–4 lbs	—	1–1½ hrs	1½–1¾ hrs
Double loin	3–5 lbs	—	1½–1¾ hrs	1¾–2½ hrs

CHOPS

Place chops on the cooking grill. Grill for the time given in the chart or till desired doneness, turning once halfway through grilling time.

Charcoal: Direct (pages 6-7)
Gas: Indirect/Medium Heat (pages 8-9)

CUT	THICKNESS	APPROXIMATE COOKING TIME		
		RARE 140°F (60°C)	MEDIUM 160°F (71°C)	WELL-DONE 170°F (77°C)
Loin and rib	1 in.	7–9 min	10–13 min	14–17 min
	1½ in.	10–13 min	14–17 min	18–21 min
Shoulder	1 in.	8–10 min	11–14 min	15–18 min
and sirloin	1½ in.	13–16 min	17–19 min	20–22 min

ROASTS

Insert a meat thermometer into the meat. Place meat, fat side up, in center of the cooking grill. Grill Indirect for the time given in the chart or till thermometer registers the desired internal temperature.

Charcoal: Indirect (pages 6-7)
Gas: Indirect/Medium Heat (pages 8-9)

CUT	WEIGHT	APPROXIMATE COOKING TIME		
		RARE 140°F (60°C)	MEDIUM 160°F (71°C)	WELL-DONE 170°F (77°C)
Leg of lamb, butterflied	4 lbs	45–55 min	55–65 min	65–75 min
Leg roast				
Boneless, rolled	5–7 lbs	1½–2¼ hrs	2¼–3 hrs	3–3½ hrs
Whole	5–7 lbs	1½–2 hrs	2–2½ hrs	2½–2¾ hrs
Rib crown roast	3–4 lbs	1–1¼ hrs	1¼–1½ hrs	1½–1¾ hrs
Rib roast	2½–3 lbs	1–1¼ hrs	1¼–1½ hrs	1½–1¾ hrs

GRILLING GUIDE FOR VEAL

CHOPS

Place chops on the cooking grill. Grill for the time given in the chart or till desired doneness, turning once halfway through grilling time.

Charcoal: Direct (pages 6-7)
Gas: Indirect/Medium Heat (pages 8-9)

CUT	THICKNESS	APPROXIMATE COOKING TIME	
		MEDIUM 160°F (71°C)	WELL-DONE 170°F (77°C)
Chops Rib and loin	¾ in.	9–11 min	11–13 min

ROASTS

Insert a meat thermometer into the meat. Place meat, fat side up, in center of cooking grill. Grill Indirect for time given in chart or till thermometer registers desired internal temperature.

Charcoal: Indirect (pages 6-7)
Gas: Indirect/Medium Heat (pages 8-9)

CUT	WEIGHT	APPROXIMATE COOKING TIME	
		MEDIUM 160°F (71°C)	WELL-DONE 170°F (77°C)
Leg round roast	3–4 lbs	1¾–2¼ hrs	2¼–2¾ hrs
Loin Roast	3 lbs	1¼–1¾ hrs	1¾–2¼ hrs
	4–6 lbs	1¾–2¼ hrs	2¼–2¾ hrs
Shoulder roast Boneless, rolled	2½–3½ lbs	1¼–1¾ hrs	1¾–2½ hrs

GRILLING GUIDE FOR GROUND MEATS

PATTIES AND SAUSAGE

Place patties and sausage on the cooking grill. Grill for the time given in the chart or till desired doneness, turning once halfway through grilling time.

Charcoal: Direct (pages 6-7)
Gas: Indirect/Medium Heat (pages 8-9)

CUT	THICKNESS	APPROXIMATE COOKING TIME	
		MEDIUM 160°F (71°C)	WELL-DONE 170°F (77°C)

Patties
  Lean ground beef,
    lamb, and pork
	¾ in.	9–10 min	11–12 min

Sausage
  Fresh bratwurst,
    Italian, and Polish
	—	—	18–25 min

BONELESS BREASTS, TURKEY PATTIES, AND TURKEY TENDERLOIN STEAKS

Place on cooking grill. Grill for the time given in chart, turning once halfway through grilling time.

Charcoal: Direct (pages 6-7)
Gas: Indirect/Medium Heat (pages 8-9)

TYPE OF POULTRY	THICKNESS/ WEIGHT	APPROXIMATE COOKING TIME MEDIUM 170°F (77°C)	WELL-DONE 180°F (82°C)
Chicken breasts, skinned and boned	4–5 oz ea	—	10–12 min
Turkey patties (ground raw turkey)	¾ in. thick	—	10–12 min
Turkey tenderloin steaks	4–6 oz ea	—	10–12 min

POULTRY PIECES AND WHOLE BIRDS

For chicken and turkey pieces, remove skin, if desired. Place, bone side down, in center of the cooking grill. Grill for the time given in the chart. During the last 10 minutes of grilling time, brush with sauce, if desired.

For a whole turkey, insert a meat thermometer in the center of the inside thigh muscle, making sure the thermometer bulb does not touch the bone. Place whole chicken or turkey, breast side up, in center of the cooking grill. Grill for the time given in the chart or till thermometer registers 180°F (82°C).

Charcoal: Indirect (pages 6-7)
Gas: Indirect/Medium Heat (pages 8-9)

TYPE OF POULTRY	THICKNESS/ WEIGHT	APPROXIMATE COOKING TIME MEDIUM 170°F (77°C)	WELL-DONE 180°F (82°C)
Broiler-fryer chicken, halves	1¼–1½ lbs	—	1–1¼ hrs
Broiler-fryer chicken, whole	3–4 lbs	—	1¼–1¾ hrs
	4–5 lbs	—	1¾–2 hrs
	5–6 lbs	—	2–2½ hrs
Chicken breast halves, thighs, and drumsticks	2–2½ lbs total	—	50–60 min
Cornish game hens, halves	½–¾ lb ea	—	40–50 min
Cornish game hens, whole	1–1½ lbs ea	—	45–60 min
Turkey, boneless, whole	2½–3½ lbs	—	1¾–2¼ hrs
Turkey, *unstuffed, whole	6–8 lbs	—	1¼–2 hrs
	10–12 lbs	—	2–3 hrs
	14–18 lbs	—	3–4 hrs
Turkey breasts, half	3–4 lbs	1½–2 hrs	—
Turkey breasts, whole	4–6 lbs	1½–2¼ hrs	—
	6–8 lbs	2–3½ hrs	—
Turkey drumsticks	½–1½ lbs ea	—	¾–1¼ hrs
Turkey hindquarters	2–4 lbs ea	—	1–1½ hrs
Turkey tenderloin, whole	1 in. thick	—	14–15 min
Turkey thigh	1–1½ lbs	—	50–60 min

*Be sure to fully defrost turkey before grilling. When defrosting turkey in the refrigerator, allow 24 hours for every 5 lbs.

FISH FILLETS AND STEAKS

Thaw fish, if frozen. Place ¼- to ½-inch-thick fish fillets on lightly greased heavy foil or in a lightly greased foil pan. Place on cooking grill. Grill for the time given in the chart or till fish flakes when tested with a fork. Place 1- to 1¼-inch-thick fish steaks on a lightly greased cooking grill. Grill for the time given in the chart or till fish flakes, turning once halfway through grilling time.

Charcoal: Direct (pages 6-7)
Gas: Indirect/Medium Heat (pages 8-9)

TYPE	THICKNESS	APPROXIMATE COOKING TIME
Fish fillets	¼–½ in.	3–5 min
	½–1 in.	6–10 min
Fish steaks	1–1¼ in.	10–12 min

WHOLE FISH

Thaw fish, if frozen.
Unstuffed fish: Place fish in center of the lightly greased cooking grill. Grill Indirect for the time given in the chart or till fish flakes when tested with a fork.
Stuffed fish: Lightly spoon hot stuffing into fish cavity. Place fish on piece of lightly greased heavy foil or in a lightly greased foil pan. Place in center of the cooking grill. Grill Indirect for the time given in the chart or till fish flakes when tested with a fork and stuffing is heated through 165°F (74°C).

Charcoal: Indirect (pages 6-7)
Gas: Indirect/Medium Heat (pages 8-9)

TYPE	WEIGHT	APPROXIMATE COOKING TIME
Whole, unstuffed	1 lb	20–25 min
	1½–2 lbs	25–30 min
	2–4 lbs	30–50 min
	4–4½ lbs	50–60 min
Whole, stuffed	9–10 oz	12–15 min
	2 lbs	50–60 min

SEAFOOD

Thaw seafood, if frozen.
Lobster tails: Place, meaty side up, on cooking grill. Grill for the time given in the chart or till meat becomes opaque.
Shrimp: Place shelled and deveined shrimp on heavy foil or in Weber® aluminum pan. Grill for the time given in the chart or till shrimp turn pink.

Charcoal: Direct (pages 6-7)
Gas: Indirect/Medium Heat (pages 8-9)

TYPE	WEIGHT	APPROXIMATE COOKING TIME
Lobster tails	5 oz	5–6 min
	10 oz	10–12 min
Shrimp, large	1 lb	4–5 min

COOKING DIRECTIONS (FOIL PACKET)

Cut an 18-inch square of heavy foil. Place vegetable in center of the foil. Season to taste with salt and pepper. Dot with margarine or butter. Add 1 tablespoon water. Bring up 2 opposite edges of foil and, leaving a little space for expansion of steam, tightly seal top, then seal

each end. Place foil packet on cooking grill. Grill Indirect for the time given in the chart, turning packet over once halfway through grilling time. Timings below are for crisp-tender vegetables. If you prefer more tender vegetables, allow longer cooking times.

VEGETABLES*	AMOUNT	APPROXIMATE COOKING TIME
Beans, green and wax (whole)	30	30–35 min.
Broccoli flowerets	1 cup	15–18 min
Brussels sprouts	1½ cups	18–20 min
Carrots (cut into ½-inch slices)	1½ cups	15–20 min
Cauliflower flowerets	2 cups	20–25 min
Corn on the cob (foil-wrapped)*	4 medium ears	25–35 min
Eggplant (cut into 1-inch slices)	1 small	20–25 min
Kohlrabi (cut into julienne strips)	1½ cups	25–30 min
Mushrooms (whole or sliced)	1½ cups	8–12 min
Peppers, sweet red, green, or yellow (cut into 1-inch strips)	1½ cups	15–20 min
Potatoes (foil-wrapped)	4 medium	50–60 min
Yellow summer squash (cut into 1-inch cubes)	1½ cups	6–10 min
Zucchini (cut into ½-inch slices)	1½ cups	6–10 min

*Note: See tip on page 131 for grilling vegetables Direct, and tip on page 125 for grilling corn on the cob.

INTERNAL FOOD TEMPERATURES

Fahrenheit (F)	Celsius (C)
140°	60°
150°	66°
160°	71°
170°	77°
180°	82°

WEBER® GRILL TEMPERATURES

Fahrenheit(F)	Celsius(C)
325°	163°
350°	177°
375°	191°
400°	204°
450°	232°
500°	260°
550°	288°

METRIC EQUIVALENTS

U.S.	Metric
1 cup	250 milliliters
1 tablespoon	20 milliliters
1 teaspoon	5 milliliters

NUTRITION INFORMATION

With each recipe we give important nutrition information. The calorie count of each serving and amount, in grams, of protein, carbohydrate, fat, cholesterol, and sodium help you keep tabs on what you eat. This is how the nutrition information was calculated:

• When ingredient options appear in the recipe, we used the first choice for the analysis.
• We omitted optional ingredients from the analysis (such as garnishes or serving suggestions).
• We based the nutrition analysis on the first serving size if a recipe gives variable serving sizes.
• For recipes with variations, we included nutrition analysis for just the primary recipe.

TENDER, JUICY MEATS

23

STEAK

Charcoal: Direct (pages 6-7)
Gas: Indirect/Medium Heat (pages 8-9)

> Beef top loin, tenderloin, T-bone, porterhouse, sirloin, rib, *or* rib eye steaks, cut 1 inch thick

Trim fat from steaks. If desired, season steaks with salt and pepper. Place steaks on the cooking grill. Grill 6 to 7 minutes for rare, 7 to 9 minutes for medium, or 9 to 11 minutes for well-done, turning once halfway through grilling time.

Note: For 1½-inch-thick steaks, allow 10 to 12 minutes for rare, 12 to 15 minutes for medium, or 15 to 19 minutes for well-done.

Per Serving (¼-pound top loin steak): 201 calories, 28 g. protein, 0 g. carbohydrate, 9 g. fat, 76 mg. cholesterol, 67 mg. sodium.

HOW MUCH STEAK TO BUY

When buying beef steak, remember that cuts with more bone and fat will give you fewer servings per pound. Count on 1 or 2 servings per pound of T-bone steak; 2 or 3 servings per pound of porterhouse, sirloin, rib, and rib eye steak; and 3 or 4 servings per pound of tenderloin or top loin steaks.

SAVORY HERBED STEAK

Charcoal: Direct (pages 6-7)
Gas: Indirect/Medium Heat (pages 8-9)

> 4 beef top loin *or* tenderloin steaks, cut 1 inch thick (1¼ pounds total)
> 1½ teaspoons dried basil, crushed
> 1 teaspoon dried tarragon, crushed
> 1 teaspoon dried snipped chives
> 4 cloves garlic, minced

Trim fat from steaks. Combine basil, tarragon, chives, and garlic. Rub herb mixture on both sides of steaks, pressing into surface. Place steaks on the cooking grill. Grill 6 to 7 minutes for rare, 7 to 9 minutes for medium, or 9 to 11 minutes for well-done, turning once halfway through grilling time. Makes 4 servings.

Per Serving: 222 calories, 31 g. protein, 1 g. carbohydrate, 10 g. fat, 81 mg. cholesterol, 72 mg. sodium.

BLUE CHEESE STEAK

Charcoal: Direct (pages 6-7)
Gas: Indirect/Medium Heat (pages 8-9)

> 1 cup crumbled blue cheese (4 ounces)
> ¼ cup thinly sliced green onions
> 4 beef top loin *or* tenderloin steaks, cut 1 inch thick (1¼ pounds total)

Combine blue cheese and green onions; set aside. Trim fat from steaks. Place steaks on the cooking grill. Grill 6 to 7 minutes for rare, 7 to 9 minutes for medium, or 9 to 11 minutes for well-done, turning once halfway through grilling time. Sprinkle with blue cheese mixture during the last half of grilling. Makes 4 servings.

Per Serving: 317 calories, 37 g. protein, 1 g. carbohydrate, 18 g. fat, 102 mg. cholesterol, 467 mg. sodium.

STEAK AU POIVRE

Charcoal: Direct (pages 6-7)
Gas: Indirect/Medium Heat (pages 8-9)

  4 beef top loin *or* tenderloin steaks, cut
      1 inch thick (1¼ pounds total)
  1 to 2 tablespoons cracked whole
      black pepper
  ¼ teaspoon salt
  1 shallot *or* 2 green onions, chopped
  ¼ cup margarine *or* butter
  ¼ cup cognac
  ¼ cup whipping cream
  2 teaspoons Dijon-style mustard

Trim fat from steaks. Combine pepper and salt. Sprinkle both sides of steaks with pepper mixture; press into surface.

Place steaks on the cooking grill. Grill 6 to 7 minutes for rare, 7 to 9 minutes for medium, or 9 to 11 minutes for well-done, turning once halfway through grilling time.

Meanwhile, in a large heavy skillet cook shallot in margarine till tender but not brown. In a small saucepan heat cognac till it almost simmers.

Transfer grilled steaks to skillet. (If desired, pour heated cognac into a large ladle.) Carefully ignite cognac and pour over steaks. Transfer steaks to a serving platter. Stir cream and mustard into cognac mixture in skillet. Pour cognac sauce over steaks. Makes 4 servings.

Note: Use the larger amount of pepper if you wish the traditional peppery bite of this dish. For milder flavor, go with the smaller amount.

Per Serving: 412 calories, 31 g. protein, 7 g. carbohydrate, 26 g. fat, 102 mg. cholesterol, 423 mg. sodium.

THREE-PEPPER STEAK

Charcoal: Direct (pages 6-7)
Gas: Indirect/Medium Heat (pages 8-9)

  2 1-pound beef porterhouse *or* T-bone
      steaks, cut 1½ inches thick
  1 teaspoon whole black peppercorns
  1 teaspoon white peppercorns
  1 teaspoon Szechuan peppercorns
  ⅛ teaspoon ground allspice

Trim fat from steaks. Coarsely crush peppercorns on a cloth with a rolling pin or with a mortar and pestle. Combine crushed peppercorns and allspice. Sprinkle both sides of steak with the pepper mixture; press into surface.

Place steaks on the cooking grill. Grill 10 to 12 minutes for rare, 12 to 15 minutes for medium, or 15 to 19 minutes for well-done; turn once halfway through grilling time. Serves 4.

Garlic Steak: Prepare as above, *except* omit peppercorn mixture. Cut 2 large cloves of *garlic* into 4 or 6 pieces. With a sharp knife cut 4 or 6 slits in side edge of *each* steak, cutting through to the center (see tip below). Stuff a garlic piece into *each* slit and grill steaks as above.

Per Serving: 247 calories, 32 g. protein, 1 g. carbohydrate, 12 g. fat, 91 mg. cholesterol, 75 mg. sodium.

FLAVOR-PACKED STEAK

To boost the flavor of steak even more, refrigerate it, covered, 1 to 2 hours after you rub it with an herb or peppercorn mixture or stuff it with garlic.

For *Garlic Steak,* use a sharp knife to cut several slits in the side edge of each steak, cutting through to the center as shown above. Then stuff a garlic piece into each slit.

STEAK SANDWICH

Charcoal: Direct (pages 6-7)
Gas: Indirect/Medium Heat (pages 8-9)

¼ cup mayonnaise *or* salad dressing
¼ cup plain yogurt
1 tablespoon Dijon-style mustard
1 1- to 1¼-pound beef flank steak
2 cloves garlic, minced
½ teaspoon salt
¼ teaspoon pepper
1 16-ounce loaf unsliced French bread
¼ cup margarine *or* butter, softened

For mustard sauce, in a small bowl combine mayonnaise, yogurt, and mustard. Cover and refrigerate till serving time. Rub meat with garlic. Season with salt and pepper. Place steak on the cooking grill. Grill 10 to 12 minutes or till outside is well browned and inside is rare, turning once halfway through grilling time. Transfer steak to a serving platter. Keep warm.

Split the bread lengthwise. Spread margarine on the cut surfaces. Place, cut side down, on the outside edge of the grill to toast lightly. To serve, slice steak diagonally across the grain into thin slices. Pile steak slices on bottom half of the toasted bread. Pour mustard sauce over beef slices. Replace top of bread. Makes 6 servings.

Barbecued Steak Sandwich: Prepare as above, *except* substitute ½ cup of bottled *barbecue sauce* for the mustard sauce.

Italian Pepper Steak Sandwich: Prepare as above, *except* omit the mustard sauce, garlic, salt, and pepper. Marinate steak in mixture of ¼ cup *vegetable oil,* 2 tablespoons *lemon juice,* 1 tablespoon *soy sauce,* 2 cloves minced *garlic,* 3 tablespoons thinly sliced *green onions,* and ¼ teaspoon bottled *hot pepper sauce* several hours or overnight. Drain beef, reserving marinade. In a medium saucepan bring reserved marinade to boiling. Add 1 medium *sweet red* or *green pepper,* cut into strips. Simmer, covered, 7 minutes or till pepper is crisp-tender. Grill meat and bread, and assemble sandwich as directed above, pouring pepper mixture over sliced meat.

Per Serving: 499 calories, 22 g. protein, 40 g. carbohydrate, 26 g. fat, 46 mg. cholesterol, 888 mg. sodium.

CARNE ASADA BARBECUE

Charcoal: Direct (pages 6-7)
Gas: Indirect/Medium Heat (pages 8-9)

1 cup lime juice
½ cup vegetable juice cocktail
¼ cup chopped onion
1 tablespoon snipped fresh parsley *or* 1 teaspoon dried parsley flakes
2 cloves garlic, minced
½ teaspoon salt
¼ teaspoon pepper
1 1½-pound beef flank steak
2 sweet red *or* green peppers, cut into thin strips
1 large onion, thinly sliced
1 tablespoon margarine *or* butter
12 8-inch flour tortillas
¾ cup salsa
1 6-ounce container frozen avocado dip, thawed

For marinade, combine lime juice, vegetable juice cocktail, chopped onion, parsley, garlic, salt, and pepper. Place steak in a plastic bag set into a shallow dish. Pour marinade over steak. Close bag. Marinate in the refrigerator 3 to 4 hours, turning bag occasionally to distribute marinade.

Meanwhile, cut an 18-inch square of heavy foil. Place peppers and sliced onion in center of foil. Dot with margarine. Bring up 2 opposite edges of foil and, leaving a little space for expansion of steam, tightly seal top, then each end.

Drain steak, reserving marinade. Place steak on the cooking grill. Grill 10 to 15 minutes for rare or 15 to 19 minutes for medium, turning and brushing with reserved marinade once halfway through grilling time. Place foil packet of vegetables on the cooking grill beside steak during the last 10 minutes of grilling time.

Wrap tortillas in heavy foil; place on cooking grill beside steak during the last 5 minutes of grilling time. Turn tortilla packet once halfway through grilling. Slice steak diagonally across the grain into thin slices. Serve in tortillas with peppers and onions, salsa, and avocado dip. Makes 6 servings.

Per Serving: 519 calories, 29 g. protein, 51 g. carbohydrate, 25 g. fat, 60 mg. cholesterol, 809 mg. sodium.

BARBECUED SHORT RIBS

Charcoal: Indirect (pages 6-7)
Gas: Indirect/Medium Heat (pages 8-9)

  4 pounds meaty beef chuck short ribs, cut
      into serving-size pieces
  1 cup bottled barbecue sauce *or*
      sweet-and-sour sauce

Trim fat from meat. Place ribs in center of the
cooking grill. Grill 1¼ to 1½ hours or till tender,
brushing with sauce during the last 20 minutes of
grilling time. Makes 4 servings.

Note: Small rib pieces will grill in less time.

*Per Serving: 417 calories, 40 g. protein, 6 g.
carbohydrate, 25 g. fat, 119 mg. cholesterol,
585 mg. sodium.*

PEANUTTY-SAUCED SHORT RIBS

Charcoal: Indirect (pages 6-7)
Gas: Indirect/Medium Heat (pages 8-9)

  ⅓ cup cooking oil
  ⅓ cup peanut butter
  2 tablespoons soy sauce
  1 tablespoon curry powder
  2 cloves garlic, minced
  ⅛ to ¼ teaspoon ground red pepper
  ½ of a 6-ounce can (⅓ cup) frozen limeade
      concentrate, thawed
  4 pounds meaty beef chuck short ribs, cut
      into serving-size pieces

For sauce, combine oil, peanut butter, soy sauce,
curry powder, garlic, and red pepper. Stir in
limeade concentrate.

Trim fat from meat. Place ribs in center of the
cooking grill. Grill 1¼ to 1½ hours or till tender,
brushing with sauce during the last 20 minutes of
grilling time. Makes 4 servings.

*Per Serving: 713 calories, 46 g. protein, 16 g.
carbohydrate, 52 g. fat, 119 mg. cholesterol,
676 mg. sodium.*

TEXAS SHORT RIBS

Charcoal: Indirect (pages 6-7)
Gas: Indirect/Medium Heat (pages 8-9)

  2 tablespoons Worcestershire sauce
  1 tablespoon cooking oil
  1 tablespoon vinegar
  ½ teaspoon instant beef bouillon granules
  1 clove garlic, minced
  ¼ to ½ teaspoon ground red pepper
  ¼ teaspoon dry mustard
  ¼ teaspoon chili powder
  4 pounds meaty beef chuck short ribs, cut
      into serving-size pieces
  1 tablespoon brown sugar
  1 teaspoon cornstarch
  ¼ cup catsup

For brushing sauce, combine Worcestershire
sauce, oil, vinegar, bouillon, garlic, red pepper,
mustard, chili powder, and ⅓ cup *water*.
Reserve ¼ *cup* of the brushing sauce; set aside.

Place ribs in center of the cooking grill. Grill
1¼ to 1½ hours or till tender, brushing
occasionally with brushing sauce.

Meanwhile, in a small saucepan combine brown
sugar and cornstarch. Stir in the ¼ cup reserved
brushing sauce and catsup. Cook and stir till
thickened and bubbly. Cook and stir 2 minutes
more. Serve with ribs. Makes 4 servings.

*Per Serving: 452 calories, 40 g. protein, 11 g.
carbohydrate, 27 g. fat, 119 mg. cholesterol,
455 mg. sodium.*

Entertain with ease.
Assemble *Oriental
Steak Pinwheels*
ahead and marinate.
Then grill and serve
over fried rice
noodles.

ORIENTAL STEAK PINWHEELS

Charcoal: Direct (pages 6-7)
Gas: Indirect/Medium Heat (pages 8-9)

 ¼ cup packed brown sugar
 ¼ cup teriyaki sauce
 1 tablespoon rice wine vinegar *or* white
    wine vinegar
 ½ teaspoon five-spice powder
 ½ teaspoon bottled minced garlic
 ¼ teaspoon ground ginger
 1 1- to 1¼-pound boneless beef top round
    steak, cut about ¾ inch thick
 2 sweet yellow *and/or* green peppers, cut
    into 1½-inch squares
    Fried rice noodles (optional)

For marinade, in a small bowl combine brown
sugar, teriyaki sauce, vinegar, five-spice powder,
garlic, and ginger; set aside.

Use a meat mallet to pound beef to ¼- to
½-inch thickness. Brush about *2 tablespoons* of
the marinade over beef. Roll up from long side.
Cut into 1-inch slices. Thread beef pinwheels and
peppers alternately onto 4 or 5 skewers. Place in
shallow baking dish. Pour remaining marinade
over. Cover and marinate in refrigerator 6 hours
or overnight, turning skewers occasionally.

Remove skewers from marinade, reserving
marinade. Place skewers on the cooking grill. Grill
9 to 11 minutes for medium or 11 to 14 minutes
for well-done, turning once and brushing with
marinade halfway through grilling time. Serve
with fried rice noodles, if desired. Serves 4.

Note: To fry rice noodles, heat deep hot cooking
oil to 375°F (191°C). Fry unsoaked noodles, a
few at a time, about 5 seconds or just till noodles
puff and rise to the top. Remove noodles; drain
on paper towels. Keep warm in oven.

*Per Serving: 241 calories, 26 g. protein, 19 g.
carbohydrate, 7 g. fat, 69 mg. cholesterol,
754 mg. sodium.*

BEEF TENDERLOIN WITH MUSHROOM-SHERRY SAUCE

Charcoal: Indirect (pages 6-7)
Gas: Indirect/Medium Heat (pages 8-9)

 1 2½- to 3-pound beef tenderloin
 ¾ teaspoon salt
 ¼ teaspoon pepper
 2 cups sliced fresh mushrooms
 1 cup sliced green onions
 ¼ cup margarine *or* butter
 2 tablespoons dry sherry
 1 tablespoon soy sauce
 1 tablespoon Dijon-style mustard

Sprinkle meat with salt and pepper. Insert a meat
thermometer into center of roast. Place roast in
center of cooking grill. Grill 45 to 60 minutes or
till meat thermometer registers 140°F (60°C). Let
stand 15 minutes. Thinly slice across the grain.

Meanwhile, for sauce, cook mushrooms and
green onions in margarine till tender. Stir in
sherry, soy sauce, and mustard. Heat through.
Serve over meat. Makes 8 servings.

Note: Pictured on page 23.

*Per Serving: 350 calories, 28 g. protein, 2 g.
carbohydrate, 24 g. fat, 91 mg. cholesterol,
520 mg. sodium.*

EASY, ELEGANT GARNISHES

**Make your roast look
extra special with one
of these garnishes.**
  Fluted mushrooms:
**With a sharp paring
knife held at an
angle, and beginning
at the top of each
mushroom cap, make
cuts in the form of a
V. Turn mushroom
slightly; cut another
V; repeat around cap.
Or, for a similar
effect, use a punch-** **type can opener to
make a series of
slight indentations
around the center of
the cap (pictured on
page 32).**
  Onion brushes:
**Remove roots and
most of the green
portion from the
ends of green onions.
Slash both ends of
onion pieces to make
fringes. Place in ice
water to curl ends.**

STANDING RIB ROAST

Charcoal: Indirect (pages 6-7)
Gas: Indirect/Medium Heat (pages 8-9)

   1 **4-pound beef rib roast**
   ¾ **teaspoon salt**
   ¼ **teaspoon pepper**

Trim fat from roast. Sprinkle with salt and pepper. Insert meat thermometer into center of roast, not touching bone. Place roast, bone side down, in center of cooking grill. Grill 1¼ to 2¼ hours for rare 140°F (60°C), 2¼ to 2¾ hours for medium 160°F (71°C), or 2¾ to 3¼ hours for well-done 170°F (77°C). Let stand 15 minutes. Serves 8.

Peppery Lemon Roast: Prepare as above, *except* omit salt and pepper. Rub roast with a mixture of 2 teaspoons *lemon-pepper seasoning* and 1 teaspoon ground *cardamom seed.*

Per Serving: 281 calories, 32 g. protein, 0 g. carbohydrate, 16 g. fat, 94 mg. cholesterol, 287 mg. sodium.

ROLLED SIRLOIN TIP ROAST

Charcoal: Indirect (pages 6-7)
Gas: Indirect/Medium Heat (pages 8-9)

   1 **3-pound sirloin tip roast**
   ½ **teaspoon salt**
   ¼ **teaspoon pepper**

Trim fat from roast. Sprinkle with salt and pepper. Insert meat thermometer into center of roast. Place roast, fat side up, in center of the cooking grill. Grill 1 to 1¾ hours for rare 140°F (60°C), 1¾ to 2¼ hours for medium 160°F (71°C), or 2¼ to 2¾ hours for well-done 170°F (77°C). Let stand 15 minutes before carving. Serves 12.

Herbed Sirloin Tip Roast: Prepare as above, *except* omit salt and pepper. Rub roast with a mixture of 1 teaspoon dried *thyme,* crushed; 1 teaspoon dried *rosemary,* crushed; 1 teaspoon dried *savory,* crushed; and ½ teaspoon *pepper.*

Per Serving: 172 calories, 24 g. protein, 0 g. carbohydrate, 8 g. fat, 65 mg. cholesterol, 146 mg. sodium.

BARBECUED BEEF BRISKET

Charcoal: Indirect (pages 6-7)
Gas: Indirect/Medium Heat (pages 8-9)

   ½ **cup red wine vinegar**
   ⅓ **cup catsup**
   2 **tablespoons Worcestershire sauce**
   2 **cloves garlic, minced**
   1 **tablespoon prepared mustard**
   ½ **teaspoon chili powder**
   ¼ **teaspoon ground red pepper**
   1 **5- to 6-pound beef brisket**
   ½ **cup catsup**
   2 **tablespoons brown sugar**
   2 **tablespoons margarine *or* butter**

Combine vinegar, ⅓ cup catsup, Worcestershire sauce, garlic, mustard, chili powder, and ground red pepper. Place brisket in plastic bag set into a shallow dish. Pour marinade over brisket. Close bag. Marinate in refrigerator several hours or overnight, turning bag several times.

Drain brisket, reserving marinade. Place brisket, fat side up, in center of the cooking grill. Brush with some of the marinade. Grill 2½ to 3 hours or till meat thermometer registers 160°F (71°C), brushing with marinade every 60 minutes.

Meanwhile, for sauce, in a small saucepan combine ½ *cup* of the reserved marinade, the ½ cup catsup, the brown sugar, and margarine. Cook and stir till bubbly. Slice brisket diagonally across the grain into thin slices. Serve with sauce. Makes 18 servings.

Build-Your-Own Brisket Sandwiches: Prepare as above, *except* serve brisket and sauce in a sandwich buffet with 1½ dozen *hamburger buns* and assorted toppers, such as sliced *sweet red* or *green peppers,* sliced *red onions,* or sliced *tomatoes.* (Pictured on pages 4-5.)

Note: To prepare charcoal grill, start with 5 fewer charcoal briquettes on *each* side for slower heat. Fill drip pan half full of water. Then add 5 briquettes to *each* side every hour to maintain temperature. For succulent smoked flavor, grill meat with mesquite or hickory wood.

Per Serving: 262 calories, 28 g. protein, 6 g. carbohydrate, 14 g. fat, 88 mg. cholesterol, 247 mg. sodium.

BOURBON STREET CHUCK ROAST

Charcoal: Indirect (pages 6-7)
Gas: Indirect/Medium Heat (pages 8-9)

1½   cups water
⅔   cup soy sauce
½   cup bourbon
¼   cup packed brown sugar
3   tablespoons Worcestershire sauce
2   tablespoons lemon juice
1   4- to 5-pound beef chuck pot roast,
      cut 1½ to 2 inches thick

For marinade, stir together water, soy sauce, bourbon, brown sugar, Worcestershire sauce, and lemon juice.

Trim fat from beef. Place beef in a plastic bag set into a shallow dish. Pour marinade over beef. Close bag. Marinate in the refrigerator 8 hours or overnight, turning bag several times to distribute the marinade.

Drain beef, reserving marinade. Insert a meat thermometer into the center of the roast. Place beef in center of the cooking grill. Grill 1 to 1¼ hours for rare 140°F (60°C), 1¼ to 1¾ hours for medium 160°F (71°C), or 1¾ to 2 hours for well-done 170°F (77°C).

Transfer beef to serving platter. Let stand 15 minutes. Thinly slice beef across the grain. Makes 10 to 12 servings.

Per Serving: 368 calories, 36 g. protein, 8 g. carbohydrate, 17 g. fat, 120 mg. cholesterol, 1,235 mg. sodium.

BRANDIED SIRLOIN TIP ROAST

Charcoal: Indirect (pages 6-7)
Gas: Indirect/Medium Heat (pages 8-9)

½   cup vegetable oil
¼   cup brandy
¼   cup apple juice
¼   cup Worcestershire sauce
2   cloves garlic, minced
¼   teaspoon pepper
1   3½-pound boneless beef sirloin tip roast

For marinade, combine oil, brandy, apple juice, Worcestershire sauce, garlic, and pepper.

Place beef in a plastic bag set into a shallow dish. Pour marinade over beef. Close bag. Marinate in refrigerator 8 hours or overnight, turning bag several times to distribute marinade.

Drain beef, reserving marinade. Insert meat thermometer into the center of the roast. Place beef in center of the cooking grill. Grill 1 to 1¾ hours for rare 140°F (60°C), 1¾ to 2¼ hours for medium 160°F (71°C), or 2¼ to 2¾ hours for well-done 170°F (77°C).

Transfer beef to a serving platter. Let stand 15 minutes before carving. Serves 8 to 10.

Per Serving: 437 calories, 41 g. protein, 6 g. carbohydrate, 26 g. fat, 108 mg. cholesterol, 178 mg. sodium.

EASY ROASTING

Here's a grill accessory you can use in your conventional oven: the Weber® Grill Works™ Roast Holder. This heavy, nickel-plated steel holder has handles that make placing and removing a roast neat and easy, whether it's on the grill or in a roasting pan in the oven.

A FRENCH DINNER PARTY

Cheese and Fruit Tray

*Burgundy Beef Roast

*Gingered Carrots and Onions

Tossed Greens

French Bread

*Peach-Raspberry Sauce with Ice Cream

Burgundy Wine

Beef and red wine are a robust flavor combination discovered long ago by skilled French cooks. Enjoy the classic pair in this elegant patio dinner. Give *Burgundy Beef Roast* an herb rub for subtle flavor, then cook it on the grill to the doneness you prefer. Cook *Gingered Carrots and Onions* and *Peach-Raspberry Sauce* on the grill, too. What an easy way to prepare a superb meal!

*Recipe included

BURGUNDY AND BEEF

French cooking is world famous, but most of us think first of the elaborate classic cuisine prepared for restaurant diners by professional chefs. Provincial cooking is home cooking, done all over the country using the finest local ingredients. The home cooks shop each day to ensure freshness.

In Burgundy in eastern France, the local products include excellent red wine and lean beef from grass-fed Charolais cattle. The sauces served with beef often are made with wine, which is also served in the glass with the meal.

Farther south, near the Mediterranean, grape-growers began the practice of adding grapevine clippings to their charcoal fire for grilling. Then an imaginative chef threw in a handful of fresh herbs to add even more flavor.

BURGUNDY BEEF ROAST

Charcoal: Indirect (pages 6-7)
Gas: Indirect/Medium Heat (pages 8-9)

    1 tablespoon cracked black pepper
   ¼ teaspoon dried thyme, crushed
   ¼ teaspoon dried marjoram, crushed
   ⅛ teaspoon ground cloves
   ⅛ teaspoon fennel seed, crushed
    1 3½- to 4-pound beef rib eye roast
 1½ cups sliced mushrooms (4 ounces)
   ½ cup finely chopped onion
    1 clove garlic, minced
    1 tablespoon olive *or* cooking oil
   ½ cup beef broth
   ¼ cup burgundy
    2 teaspoons cornstarch
   ¼ cup butter, softened
    8 medium mushroom caps (optional)

Combine pepper, thyme, marjoram, cloves, and fennel seed. Rub pepper mixture over all sides of roast. Place roast in center of the cooking grill. Grill 1 to 1¼ hours for rare 140°F (60°C), 1¼ to 1½ hours for medium 160°F (71°C), or 1½ to 1¾ hours for well-done 170°F (77°C). Cover and let stand 15 minutes before carving.

Meanwhile, for the mushroom sauce, in a 10-inch skillet cook the sliced mushrooms, onion, and garlic in hot oil till vegetables are tender. Combine broth, burgundy, and cornstarch. Add to skillet. Cook and stir till thickened and bubbly. Cook and stir 1 minute more. Remove from heat. Blend in butter, *1 tablespoon* at a time. Serve with roast. Garnish with fluted mushroom caps, if desired. Serves 8.

Note: For instructions on fluting mushroom caps, see "Easy, Elegant Garnishes" on page 29. Pictured on page 32.

Per Serving: 407 calories, 37 g. protein, 3 g. carbohydrate, 26 g. fat, 123 mg. cholesterol, 199 mg. sodium.

GINGERED CARROTS AND ONIONS

Charcoal: Indirect (pages 6-7)
Gas: Indirect/Medium Heat (pages 8-9)

- 1 pound baby carrots *or* 6 medium carrots, cut into thin strips
- 1 16-ounce package frozen small whole onions, thawed and drained
- 3 tablespoons brown sugar
- 2 tablespoons butter *or* margarine, melted
- ¼ teaspoon salt
- ¼ teaspoon ground ginger
- ¼ cup chopped toasted pecans (optional)

Cut an 18x18-inch piece of heavy foil. Place carrots and onions in center of foil. Combine butter, brown sugar, salt, and ginger. Pour over carrots and onions. Bring up opposite edges of foil and, leaving a little space for expansion of steam, tightly seal top, then each end.

Place foil packet in center of the cooking grill. Grill 35 to 45 minutes or till the vegetables are tender. Remove from grill. Open packet. Sprinkle vegetables with pecans, if desired. Serve with a slotted spoon. Makes 8 servings.

Note: Pictured on page 33.

Per Serving: 84 calories, 1 g. protein, 14 g. carbohydrate, 3 g. fat, 8 mg. cholesterol, 116 mg. sodium.

PEACH-RASPBERRY SAUCE

Charcoal: Indirect (pages 6-7)
Gas: Indirect/Medium Heat (pages 8-9)

- ¾ cup seedless red raspberry preserves
- ½ teaspoon finely shredded lemon peel
- 2 tablespoons lemon juice
- 2 tablespoons butter *or* margarine, melted
- 2 tablespoons cream sherry *or* raspberry liqueur
- ⅛ teaspoon ground nutmeg
- 1 16-ounce package frozen sliced peaches, thawed
- 1 quart vanilla ice cream

In an 8x5¼-inch Weber® aluminum pan or 8x8x2-inch baking pan combine preserves, lemon peel, lemon juice, butter, sherry, and nutmeg. Stir in peaches. Cover with foil.

Place pan in center of the cooking grill. Grill 20 to 25 minutes or till sauce is heated through and peaches are tender. Serve warm sauce over scoops of ice cream. Makes 8 servings.

Note: Pictured on pages 32-33.

Per Serving: 272 calories, 3 g. protein, 44 g. carbohydrate, 10 g. fat, 37 mg. cholesterol, 86 mg. sodium.

PERFECT TIMING

One day before:
- ☐ Wash and tear greens for salad.
- ☐ Clean carrots; cover with water.
- ☐ Refrigerate onions and peaches to thaw overnight.

Before serving:
- ☐ Fire up the grill.
- ☐ Rub roast with herbs; begin grilling.
- ☐ Prepare vegetable packet; place on grill after roast has grilled one hour.
- ☐ Prepare Peach-Raspberry Sauce.

- ☐ Prepare cheese and grapes for the fruit tray.
- ☐ Finish salad.
- ☐ Slice bread.
- ☐ Slice apples and pears for fruit tray.
- ☐ Remove roast from grill; let stand. Prepare mushroom sauce for roast.
- ☐ Remove vegetable packet from grill, slice roast, and call guests to dinner.
- ☐ Grill Peach-Raspberry Sauce while eating the main course.

PORK CHOPS

Charcoal: Indirect (pages 6-7)
Gas: Indirect/Medium Heat (pages 8-9)

  4 **pork loin chops, cut 1¼ to 1½ inches thick (about 2 pounds)**
 ½ **teaspoon salt**
 ¼ **teaspoon pepper**

Trim fat from chops. Season chops with salt and pepper. Place chops in center of the cooking grill. Grill 35 to 40 minutes for medium 160°F (71°C) or 40 to 45 minutes for well-done 170°F (77°C). Makes 4 servings.

Barbecued Pork Chops: Prepare as above, *except* omit salt and pepper. Brush chops with bottled *barbecue sauce* during the last 3 minutes of grilling time.

Citrus Pork Chops: Prepare as above, *except* omit salt and pepper. Brush chops with a mixture of ⅓ cup *orange marmalade,* 2 teaspoons *soy sauce,* and dash ground *ginger* during the last 3 minutes of grilling time.

Spiced Pork Chops: Prepare as above, *except* omit salt and pepper. Brush chops with 1 tablespoon *soy sauce,* and rub with mixture of ½ teaspoon *paprika,* ¼ teaspoon *garlic salt,* ¼ teaspoon ground *ginger,* ¼ teaspoon *dry mustard,* and ¼ teaspoon *pepper* before grilling.

Per Serving: 262 calories, 36 g. protein, 1 g. carbohydrate, 12 g. fat, 112 mg. cholesterol, 355 mg. sodium.

PEPPERED APPLE CHOPS

Charcoal: Indirect (pages 6-7)
Gas: Indirect/Medium Heat (pages 8-9)

 ½ **cup apple jelly**
 2 **canned jalapeño chili peppers, chopped**
 2 **tablespoons apple juice *or* orange juice**
1½ **teaspoons cornstarch**
 4 **pork loin chops, cut 1¼ to 1½ inches thick (about 2 pounds total)**
 1 **medium apple**

In a small saucepan combine apple jelly and jalapeño peppers. Cook and stir over low heat till jelly melts. Combine apple juice and cornstarch. Stir into jelly mixture. Cook and stir till thickened and bubbly. Cook and stir for 2 minutes more.

Trim fat from chops. Place chops in center of the cooking grill. Grill 35 to 40 minutes for medium 160°F (71°C) or 40 to 45 minutes for well-done 170°F (77°C). Brush with jelly mixture during the last 10 minutes of grilling time.

Meanwhile, cut apple crosswise into two ½-inch slices. Core and halve slices; wrap in heavy foil. Place on side of grill when chops are turned. Serve apples over chops. Spoon any remaining jelly mixture over all. Makes 4 servings.

Per Serving: 388 calories, 36 g. protein, 33 g. carbohydrate, 12 g. fat, 112 mg. cholesterol, 159 mg. sodium.

PECAN-STUFFED PORK CHOPS

Charcoal: Indirect (pages 6-7)
Gas: Indirect/Medium Heat (pages 8-9)

- ¾ cup coarsely chopped pecans
- ¼ cup sliced green onions
- ¼ cup chopped green pepper
- 3 tablespoons margarine *or* butter
- ¼ teaspoon dried rosemary, crushed
- ⅛ teaspoon pepper
- 2 slices whole wheat bread, cut into ½-inch cubes (1½ cups)
- 2 tablespoons chicken broth
- 6 pork loin chops, cut 1½ inches thick (about 2½ pounds)

For pecan stuffing, in a medium skillet cook pecans, onions, and green pepper in margarine till onions are tender; stir in rosemary and pepper. Cook 1 minute more. Stir in bread cubes; toss with enough chicken broth just to moisten.

Trim fat from chops. Cut a pocket in *each* chop by cutting from fat side almost to bone. Spoon about *¼ cup* of the stuffing into *each* pork chop. Secure pockets with wooden toothpicks.

Place chops in center of the cooking grill. Grill 20 minutes. Turn and grill 20 to 25 minutes more or till no pink remains. Remove toothpicks before serving. Makes 6 servings.

Per Serving: 373 calories, 30 g. protein, 8 g. carbohydrate, 25 g. fat, 84 mg. cholesterol, 200 mg. sodium.

HONEY-BARBECUED PORK

Charcoal: Indirect (pages 6-7)
Gas: Indirect/Medium Heat (pages 8-9)

- ¼ cup catsup
- ¼ cup honey
- 3 tablespoons soy sauce
  Few dashes bottled hot pepper sauce
- 1 teaspoon dried rosemary *or* thyme, crushed
- ¼ teaspoon garlic powder
- ¼ teaspoon pepper
- 4 boneless pork loin chops, cut 1½ inches thick (1½ pounds)

For barbecue sauce, combine catsup, honey, soy sauce, and hot pepper sauce; set aside. For seasoning mixture, combine rosemary, garlic powder, and pepper.

Trim fat from chops. Sprinkle both sides of *each* chop with seasoning mixture. Place chops in center of the cooking grill. Grill 35 to 40 minutes for medium 160°F (71°C) or 40 to 45 minutes for well-done 170°F (77°C), turning once and brushing with sauce during the last 20 minutes of grilling time. Pass remaining sauce. Makes 4 servings.

Note: Try the delicious barbecue sauce in this recipe on grilled chicken or turkey, too.

Per Serving: 336 calories, 35 g. protein, 23 g. carbohydrate, 11 g. fat, 105 mg. cholesterol, 1,034 mg. sodium.

GRAB IT

To turn food on the grill without piercing it, Weber offers WeberGrabbers® Tongs. These stainless steel tongs have hardwood handles that give you the safe, sure grip you need for turning even hard-to-manage foods, like stuffed pork chops. They're also great for rearranging charcoal briquettes.

37

Chunks of cantaloupe, pineapple, and grapes sweeten the sauce that flavors these *Fruited Spareribs.*

BARBECUED PORK RIBS

Charcoal: Indirect (pages 6-7)
Gas: Indirect/Medium Heat (pages 8-9)

> 1 cup Weber Tangy Barbecue Sauce
>   (see recipe, page 113)
> 3 pounds pork loin back *or* spareribs

Prepare sauce. Place ribs in center of the cooking grill. Grill 1 to 1½ hours or till tender, brushing with sauce during the last 20 minutes of grilling time. To serve, cut ribs into 2- or 3-rib portions. Makes 4 servings.

Per Serving: 631 calories, 40 g. protein, 16 g. carbohydrate, 44 g. fat, 162 mg. cholesterol, 624 mg. sodium.

ORIENTAL RIBS

Charcoal: Indirect (pages 6-7)
Gas: Indirect/Medium Heat (pages 8-9)

> ⅓ cup soy sauce
> 2 tablespoons dry sherry
> 2 tablespoons hoisin sauce
> 1 tablespoon cooking oil
> 1 teaspoon five-spice powder
> 1 clove garlic, minced
> ¼ teaspoon pepper
> 3 pounds meaty pork spareribs *or*
>   loin back ribs

For marinade, combine soy sauce, sherry, hoisin sauce, cooking oil, five-spice powder, garlic, and pepper. Place ribs in plastic bag set into a shallow dish. Pour marinade over ribs. Close bag. Marinate in the refrigerator 4 hours or overnight, turning bag occasionally.

Drain ribs, reserving marinade. Place ribs in center of the cooking grill. Grill 1 to 1½ hours or till tender, brushing with reserved marinade during the last 20 minutes of grilling time. To serve, cut ribs into 2- or 3-rib portions. Makes 4 servings.

Per Serving: 598 calories, 41 g. protein, 5 g. carbohydrate, 44 g. fat, 163 mg. cholesterol, 1,574 mg. sodium.

FRUITED SPARERIBS

Charcoal: Indirect (pages 6-7)
Gas: Indirect/Medium Heat (pages 8-9)

> 4 to 5 pounds meaty pork spareribs *or* loin
>   back ribs
> ¼ cup sliced green onions
> 1 teaspoon grated gingerroot
> 2 tablespoons margarine *or* butter
> ½ cup pineapple preserves
> 2 cups seeded, peeled, and finely chopped
>   cantaloupe *or* peeled and chopped,
>   pitted peaches
> 2 tablespoons vinegar
> 1 tablespoon cornstarch
> ½ cup seedless green *or* red grapes, halved

Cut ribs into 2- or 3-rib portions. In saucepan cook onions and gingerroot in margarine till tender. Cut up any large pineapple pieces in preserves. Stir preserves and cantaloupe into onion mixture. Cook and stir till preserves melt. Stir vinegar and ¼ cup *water* into cornstarch. Add to onion mixture. Cook and stir till thickened and bubbly. Cook and stir 2 minutes more.

Place ribs in center of cooking grill. Grill 1 to 1½ hours or till tender, brushing with sauce during the last 20 minutes of grilling time. Place saucepan on side of grill to warm sauce; stir in grapes just before serving. Pass sauce with ribs. Makes 5 or 6 servings.

Per Serving: 737 calories, 43 g. protein, 33 g. carbohydrate, 48 g. fat, 173 mg. cholesterol, 196 mg. sodium.

RIBS IN A RACK

Neat and easy! That's the way you'll grill ribs when you use the Weber® Grill Works™ Rib Rack. Place whole or halved slabs of ribs in the rack. Then place the rack in the center of cooking grill above drip pan, and grill as directed in recipe.

By using the Grill Works Rib Rack, you increase the grilling space by 50 percent because the ribs stand up rather than lie flat on the grill. Fill the extra space with one of the vegetables featured in the "Exciting Extras" section.

WINE-BARBECUED RIBS

Charcoal: Indirect (pages 6-7)
Gas: Indirect/Medium Heat (pages 8-9)

         2 cups water
         ½ cup dry red wine
         ⅓ cup red *or* white wine vinegar
         ¼ cup catsup
         2 cloves garlic, minced
      1¼ teaspoons pepper
         1 teaspoon dry mustard
         1 teaspoon ground ginger
         1 teaspoon celery seed, crushed
         2 bay leaves
         ¼ teaspoon salt
            Several dashes bottled hot pepper sauce
         3 to 4 pounds meaty pork spareribs, cut
            into serving-size pieces
         ½ cup catsup
         ¼ cup packed brown sugar

For marinade, combine water, wine, wine vinegar, ¼ cup catsup, garlic, pepper, mustard, ginger, celery seed, bay leaves, salt, and hot pepper sauce.

Place ribs in a plastic bag set into a shallow dish. Pour marinade over ribs. Close bag. Marinate in the refrigerator 4 to 6 hours, turning bag occasionally to distribute marinade.

Drain ribs, reserving *1 cup* of the marinade. Stir ½ cup catsup and the brown sugar into reserved marinade. Place ribs in center of the cooking grill. Grill 1 to 1½ hours or till no pink remains, brushing with marinade mixture during the last 15 minutes of grilling time. Serves 4 or 5.

Per Serving: 591 calories, 34 g. protein, 29 g. carbohydrate, 34 g. fat, 137 mg. cholesterol, 656 mg. sodium.

STUFFED CROWN OF RIBS

Charcoal: Indirect (pages 6-7)
Gas: Indirect/Medium Heat (pages 8-9)

         4 pounds pork loin back ribs (2 slabs)
         ¾ cup water
         ¾ cup finely chopped celery
         1 6-ounce package mixed dried fruit bits
         ½ cup chopped onion
      1½ teaspoons instant chicken bouillon
            granules
         1 teaspoon dried basil, crushed
         ½ teaspoon dried marjoram, crushed
         ¼ teaspoon pepper
         2 tablespoons margarine *or* butter
         5 to 7 slices whole wheat bread, dried and
            cut into ½-inch cubes (4 cups)
         ¼ cup snipped fresh parsley *or* 4 teaspoons
            dried parsley flakes

To form a crown with the ribs, place slabs end to end with edges overlapping slightly and the meaty side of ribs facing toward center. Tie string securely around ribs to form a crown 8 to 9 inches in diameter.

For stuffing, in saucepan combine water, celery, dried fruit, onion, bouillon granules, basil, marjoram, and pepper. Bring to boiling; reduce heat. Cover; simmer 5 minutes. Add margarine. In bowl combine fruit mixture, bread cubes, and parsley. Toss to mix. If necessary, add additional *water* (about 2 tablespoons) to moisten mixture.

Place crown in center of the cooking grill on a double layer of greased heavy-duty foil. Spoon stuffing mixture into center of crown. Cover stuffing loosely with foil. Insert a meat thermometer into meatiest portion of ribs.

Grill 1½ to 2 hours or till meat thermometer registers 170°F (77°C) and stuffing is heated to at least 165°F (74°C). Let stand 15 minutes. To serve, transfer meat to a serving platter. Remove strings. Using a fork to steady the crown, cut between the ribs. Garnish with celery leaves and dried apricots, if desired. Makes 6 servings.

Note: Pictured on page 22.

Per Serving: 449 calories, 34 g. protein, 36 g. carbohydrate, 20 g. fat, 82 mg. cholesterol, 532 mg. sodium.

PORK LOIN ROAST

Charcoal: Indirect (pages 6-7)
Gas: Indirect/Medium Heat (pages 8-9)

  1 **4-pound boneless pork top loin roast**
     (single loin)
  ½ **teaspoon salt**
  ¼ **teaspoon pepper**

Season roast with salt and pepper. Insert meat thermometer in center of pork roast. Place roast in center of the cooking grill. Grill 1 to 1½ hours for medium 160°F (71°C) or 1½ to 1¾ hours for well-done 170°F (77°C). Makes 8 to 10 servings.

Honey-Lime Pork Roast: Prepare as above, *except* omit salt and pepper. Brush roast with a mixture of ¼ cup sliced *green onions,* ¼ cup *lime* or *lemon juice,* ¼ cup *honey,* 2 teaspoons *prepared mustard,* ½ teaspoon *salt,* and ¼ teaspoon *pepper* during the last 15 to 20 minutes of grilling time.

Note: Use limes to garnish as well as flavor the *Honey-Lime Pork Roast.* To make fanciful lime cartwheels, use a paring knife to cut long, V-shape grooves from end to end all around the lime. Then slice the lime into ⅛-inch-thick slices. Place around edge of platter.

Or, to make lime twists, first cut the lime into ⅛-inch-thick slices. Make one cut in each lime slice from the center through the rind. Twist the cut ends in opposite directions so the lime slices will stand next to the roast on a platter.

Per Serving: 366 calories, 41 g. protein, 0 g. carbohydrate, 22 g. fat, 138 mg. cholesterol, 239 mg. sodium.

ELEGANT STUFFED PORK ROAST

Charcoal: Indirect (pages 6-7)
Gas: Indirect/Medium Heat (pages 8-9)

  1 **3- to 3½-pound boneless pork top loin**
     roast (single loin)
  1 **medium onion, chopped (½ cup)**
  2 **tablespoons margarine *or* butter**
  1 **medium apple, cored, peeled, and finely**
     chopped (1 cup)
  ½ **cup soft bread crumbs**
  ⅓ **cup chopped ripe olives (optional)**
  ¼ **cup chopped boiled ham**
  ¼ **cup chopped walnuts**
  ¼ **teaspoon salt**
  ⅛ **teaspoon dried thyme, crushed**

Trim fat from meat. Using a sharp knife, slice the roast crosswise at 1-inch intervals, making *each* slice go halfway through the roast, to form 8 to 10 deep pockets in the roast.

For stuffing, in a skillet cook onion in margarine till tender. Stir in apple. Cook 1 minute more. Add bread crumbs, olives, ham, walnuts, salt, and thyme; combine well.

Generously stuff the roast, using about *3 tablespoons* of the stuffing for *each* pocket. Tie roast lengthwise around the outside at 1-inch intervals to hold the roast together.

Place roast in center of the cooking grill. Grill 2 to 2½ hours or till meat thermometer registers 160°F (71°C). Let stand 15 minutes before carving. Remove string and slice roast between pockets. Makes 8 to 10 servings.

Per Serving: 382 calories, 36 g. protein, 5 g. carbohydrate, 23 g. fat, 118 mg. cholesterol, 262 mg. sodium.

SEEDED PORK ROAST

Charcoal: Indirect (pages 6-7)
Gas: Indirect/Medium Heat (pages 8-9)

1 3½-pound boneless pork top loin roast
  (double loin tied)
3 tablespoons soy sauce
2 tablespoons aniseed
2 tablespoons fennel seed
2 tablespoons caraway seed
2 tablespoons dillseed

Trim fat from roast. Rub soy sauce over the surface of the roast with your fingers. Combine aniseed, fennel seed, caraway seed, and dillseed. Roll meat in seed mixture to coat evenly; wrap in foil and refrigerate 1 to 2 hours or overnight.

Remove foil from meat. Insert a meat thermometer near center of roast. Place roast in center of the cooking grill. Grill 1½ to 1¾ hours for medium 160°F (71°C) or 1¾ to 2½ hours for well-done 170°F (77°C). Let stand 15 minutes. Makes 8 to 10 servings.

Note: To make coating the roast easier, combine the four kinds of seeds in a 15x10x1-inch baking pan. Roll the roast in the seeds to coat it evenly. It may be necessary to press the seeds onto the surface of the roast to make them stick.

Per Serving: 334 calories, 36 g. protein, 2 g. carbohydrate, 19 g. fat, 119 mg. cholesterol, 479 mg. sodium.

ORANGE-APRICOT-GLAZED HAM

Charcoal: Indirect (pages 6-7)
Gas: Indirect/Medium Heat (pages 8-9)

¼ cup apricot preserves
¼ cup orange juice
2 tablespoons soy sauce
1 tablespoon lemon juice
1 5- to 7-pound fully cooked boneless ham
  Whole cloves

For glaze, combine apricot preserves, orange juice, soy sauce, and lemon juice.

Score ham by making shallow cuts diagonally across the surface in a diamond pattern. Stud with cloves. Insert a meat thermometer near center of ham.

Place ham in center of the cooking grill. Grill 1 to 2½ hours or till meat thermometer registers 140°F (60°C), brushing with glaze during the last 15 minutes of grilling time. Let stand 15 minutes.

Heat remaining glaze on the side of the grill to pass with ham. Just before serving, brush ham with glaze again. Makes 12 to 16 servings.

Note: For a special touch, arrange pineapple rings on top of ham before brushing with glaze.

Per Serving: 225 calories, 33 g. protein, 6 g. carbohydrate, 7 g. fat, 72 mg. cholesterol, 1,897 mg. sodium.

BEST-EVER BRATWURST

Charcoal: Indirect (pages 6-7)
Gas: Indirect/Medium Heat (pages 8-9)

  1 12-ounce can beer
  5 fresh bratwurst
  5 individual French-style rolls, halved
      lengthwise
      Desired condiments (mustard, catsup,
      pickle relish, pickled chili peppers,
      deli-style coleslaw, *or* sauerkraut)

Pour beer into a Weber® 8x5¼-inch aluminum pan. Place pan in center of the cooking grill.

Arrange bratwurst beside pan on cooking grill. Grill 6 to 8 minutes or till lightly browned, turning once halfway through grilling time. Place brats in pan of beer. Cover with foil; grill 25 minutes or till sausage juices run clear. Serve brats in rolls with desired condiments. Makes 5 servings.

Per Serving: 525 calories, 21 g. protein, 34 g. carbohydrate, 34 g. fat, 71 mg. cholesterol, 1,574 mg. sodium.

SAUSAGE SAVVY

Get a handle on what's what at the sausage counter with the help of this sausage glossary.

Bratwurst: Fresh or precooked German sausage (link) made from veal and pork.

Italian sausage: Fresh hot or mildly seasoned pork sausage. Also called pizza sausage.

Kielbasa or Polish sausage: Uncooked, smoked sausage made from coarsely ground lean pork with beef added; highly seasoned with garlic.

Knackwurst: Cooked, chunky German frankfurter highly seasoned with garlic.

Liverwurst: Finely ground, selected pork and livers. Seasoned with onions and spices; may also be smoked after cooking or may include smoked meat, such as bacon.

Pork sausage: Fresh American sausage (bulk or link) made from fresh pork and seasoned with pepper, nutmeg, sage, and other spices.

SAUSAGE SAMPLER KABOBS

Charcoal: Direct (pages 6-7)
Gas: Indirect/Medium Heat (pages 8-9)

  2 slices bacon
  ⅓ cup chopped onion
  ¼ cup chopped green pepper
  1 tablespoon all-purpose flour
  2 teaspoons sugar
      Dash pepper
  ½ cup beer
  ¼ cup water
  2 tablespoons vinegar
  8 small new potatoes (about ¾ pound)
  2 fresh bratwurst links
  2 fresh mild Italian sausage links
  2 fresh Polish sausage links

For sauce, in a skillet partially cook the bacon. Drain bacon, reserving drippings in skillet. Crumble bacon and set aside. Add onion and green pepper to drippings in skillet; cook till onion is tender but not brown. Stir in flour, sugar, and pepper. Add beer, water, and vinegar. Cook and stir till thickened and bubbly. Cook and stir 2 minutes more.

Peel a strip from the middle of *each* potato. In a saucepan precook the potatoes, covered, in enough boiling water to cover 5 minutes. Drain and set aside.

Cut *each* sausage link crosswise into 4 pieces. On four 12-inch skewers alternately thread potatoes and sausage pieces. Place on the cooking grill. Grill 20 to 25 minutes or till sausage is done and potatoes are tender, turning once and brushing with sauce halfway through grilling time. Add bacon to the remaining sauce; heat through and pass with kabobs. Makes 4 servings.

Note: You can prepare this recipe with 6 links of the same kind of sausage instead of the 3 different kinds listed.

Per Serving: 521 calories, 19 g. protein, 30 g. carbohydrate, 35 g. fat, 113 mg. cholesterol, 1,075 mg. sodium.

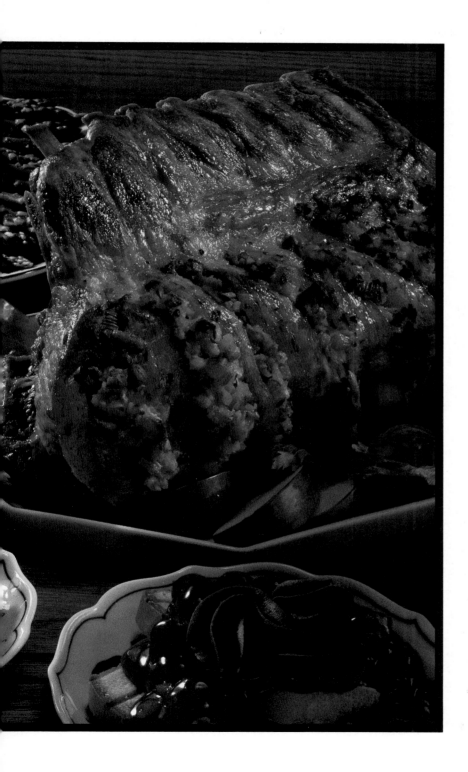

A
GERMAN
BARBECUE

*Asparagus Bundles
with Tarragon Butter

*Roast Pork with
Savory Apple Stuffing

*New Potato
Tossed Salad

*Black Forest Dessert

Beer or Iced Tea

Celebrate with an
Oktoberfest-inspired
menu. Robust and
satisfying, *Roast Pork
with Savory Apple
Stuffing* is outdoor
dining at its best. Cut
pockets in a pork loin
center rib roast and
stuff with a rye bread
and apple mixture
seasoned German-style
with caraway seed.
Asparagus Bundles are
tied with green onion
ribbons for easy
serving. Complete the
all-grilled menu with
*New Potato Tossed
Salad* and *Black
Forest Dessert.*

*Recipe included

PORK PREPARED TO PERFECTION

German cooking has a hearty "meat and potatoes" emphasis, and the national meat preference for centuries has been pork. In Cologne, archaeologists have uncovered a mosaic floor laid when the city was the northern outpost of the Roman Empire. The floor shows a merchant and his guests banqueting on wild boar. Today's favorites are roasts, chops, smoked meats, and dozens of types of sausages.

Herbs are used sparingly, but Germans enjoy caraway seed, juniper berries, and zesty coarse mustard with pork. Marinades may contain vinegar, wine, or buttermilk.

The sweet-sour taste of fruit with meat is uniquely German. Apples, pears, plums, and dried fruits flavor pork dishes, often with cider vinegar.

Stuffed meats also are a specialty of German cooks.

ROAST PORK WITH SAVORY APPLE STUFFING

Charcoal: Indirect (pages 6-7)
Gas: Indirect/Medium Heat (pages 8-9)

- ½ cup chopped onion
- ½ cup chopped celery
- 2 tablespoons margarine *or* butter
- 1½ cups finely chopped, peeled apples (2 apples)
- ¼ cup apple juice
- ¾ cup soft rye *or* pumpernickel bread cubes
- ⅓ cup chopped almonds
- ¼ teaspoon salt
- ¼ teaspoon caraway seed
- 1 4- to 5-pound pork loin center rib roast, back bone loosened (8 ribs)
  Red apple, cut into wedges (optional)
  Celery leaves (optional)

For stuffing, in a saucepan cook onion and celery in margarine till tender. Add apple juice and apples. Cover and simmer 5 minutes. Uncover and simmer 5 minutes more or till liquid evaporates. Remove from heat. Stir in bread cubes, almonds, salt, and caraway seed.

Place roast, bone side down, on a cutting board. On the meaty side, cut a pocket above *each* rib, making 8 pockets total. Spoon stuffing into pockets. Place roast with tips of ribs upward in center of the cooking grill. Cover stuffing area loosely with foil. Insert a meat thermometer into meatiest portion of roast. Grill 1 to 2¼ hours for medium 160°F (71°C) or 1¾ to 2½ hours for well-done 170°F (77°C). Remove foil halfway through grilling. Cover and let stand 10 minutes before carving. Garnish with fresh apple slices and celery leaves, if desired. Makes 8 servings.

Note: Pictured on page 45.

Per Serving: 290 calories, 24 g. protein, 8 g. carbohydrate, 18 g. fat, 77 mg. cholesterol, 184 mg. sodium.

ASPARAGUS BUNDLES WITH TARRAGON BUTTER

Charcoal: Indirect (pages 6-7)
Gas: Indirect/Medium Heat (pages 8-9)

1½ pounds fresh asparagus spears
  8 8-inch green onion leaf tops, blanched

Remove tough ends and wash asparagus. Divide into 8 bundles; tie *each* with a green onion top. Place bundles in center of cooking grill. Grill 10 minutes or till tender; turn once halfway through grilling time. Serve with Tarragon Butter. Serves 8.

Tarragon Butter: Combine ⅓ cup *butter,* 2 teaspoons snipped *tarragon,* and ¼ teaspoon each of *onion salt* and *lemon-pepper seasoning.*

Note: Pictured on pages 44-45.

Per Serving: 89 calories, 2 g. protein, 4 g. carbohydrate, 8 g. fat, 21 mg. cholesterol, 125 mg. sodium.

NEW POTATO TOSSED SALAD

Charcoal: Indirect (pages 6-7)
Gas: Indirect/Medium Heat (pages 8-9)

  1 pound new potatoes, halved *or* quartered
  1 large sweet red pepper, cut into strips
  ¼ cup sliced green onions
  ½ teaspoon celery seed
  ¼ teaspoon mustard seed
  1 8-ounce bottle clear French dressing
5½ cups torn salad greens
  ½ cup thinly sliced radishes
  ¼ cup chopped celery
  3 slices bacon, crisp-cooked and crumbled

Cook potatoes in boiling salted water 10 to 12 minutes or till tender. Drain. In a Weber® 8x5¼-inch aluminum pan combine potatoes, pepper, onions, celery seed, and mustard seed; drizzle with dressing. Cover pan with foil; place in center of cooking grill. Grill 20 to 30 minutes or till heated through. Toss together remaining ingredients. Top with hot potato mixture. Toss till slightly wilted. Serve immediately. Serves 8.

Note: Pictured on page 44.

Per Serving: 234 calories, 3 g. protein, 18 g. carbohydrate, 17 g. fat, 2 mg. cholesterol, 385 mg. sodium.

BLACK FOREST DESSERT

Charcoal: Indirect (pages 6-7)
Gas: Indirect/Medium Heat (pages 8-9)

  ¼ cup unsweetened cocoa powder
  3 tablespoons butter *or* margarine
  2 to 2½ cups sifted powdered sugar
  2 tablespoons milk
  1 teaspoon vanilla
  1 21-ounce can cherry pie filling
  ½ cup chopped toasted hazelnuts
  2 tablespoons Kirsch
16 3x2x½-inch slices pound cake

For chocolate buttercream, beat together butter and cocoa. Beat in *1 cup* powdered sugar. Add milk and vanilla. Gradually beat in enough of the remaining powdered sugar to make of piping consistency. Pipe 8 mounds on a waxed paper-lined plate; chill. In Weber 8x5¼-inch aluminum pan combine pie filling, Kirsch, and nuts. Place in center of cooking grill. Grill 15 minutes or till hot.

Place cake slices in center of cooking grill. Grill 2 to 3 minutes or till toasted, turning once. For *each* serving, arrange 2 cake slices on a plate. Top with cherry sauce and buttercream. Serves 8.

Note: Pictured on pages 44-45.

Per Serving: 488 calories, 6 g. protein, 77 g. carbohydrate, 20 g. fat, 128 mg. cholesterol, 292 mg. sodium.

PERFECT TIMING

One day before:
☐ Prepare asparagus bundles, tarragon butter, and chocolate buttercream; chill.
☐ Cook potatoes.

Before serving:
☐ Fire up the grill.
☐ Prepare and begin grilling roast.
☐ Prepare potato mixture; add to grill after roast has grilled 2 hours.

☐ Remove roast from grill; let stand. Add asparagus to grill.
☐ Prepare cherry sauce for dessert.
☐ Remove all vegetables from grill.
☐ Transfer roast and asparagus bundles to serving platters.
☐ Toss salad and call guests to dinner.
☐ Grill cherry sauce and cake slices while eating main course.

47

This attractive *Gyros Roast* actually is lamb and beef, seasoned and rolled together to form one delectable roast.

GYROS ROAST

Charcoal: Indirect (pages 6-7)
Gas: Indirect/Medium Heat (pages 8-9)

  1 3½-pound boneless leg of lamb
2½ pounds boneless beef round steak
  3 tablespoons dried oregano, crushed
  2 teaspoons dried dillweed
  2 teaspoons garlic powder
1½ teaspoons salt
  1 teaspoon pepper
  ½ teaspoon ground thyme
  3 tablespoons olive oil

With a meat mallet, pound lamb and beef into two 14x12-inch rectangles, working from center to edges and trimming as necessary. Combine oregano, dillweed, garlic powder, salt, pepper, and thyme, crushing with back of spoon or with mortar and pestle until fine textured, but not powdery. Place lamb on cutting board. Brush top with a *third* of the olive oil. Sprinkle with a *third* of the herb mixture. Using a meat mallet, pound herb mixture into surface of lamb.

Lay beef round steak on top of lamb. Brush top with a *third* of the olive oil. Sprinkle with a *third* of the herb mixture. Using a meat mallet, pound herb mixture into surface of beef.

Roll up pieces of meat as tightly as possible, starting at short end. Tie securely in several places with string. Brush outside of roast lightly with remaining olive oil. Rub remaining herb mixture on outside surface of meat. Insert meat thermometer so the tip is near center of meat.

Place roast in center of the cooking grill. Grill about 1½ hours for rare 140°F (60°C) or 1¾ hours for medium 160°F (71°C), turning roast once halfway through grilling time. (Outside of meat will become very dark and crusty.) Let stand 15 minutes. Slice thinly. Serves 12 to 16.

Note: For a more intense flavor, cover and refrigerate the seasoned roast several hours or overnight before grilling.

Per Serving: 319 calories, 43 g. protein, 1 g. carbohydrate, 16 g. fat, 131 mg. cholesterol, 369 mg. sodium.

GREEK-STYLE LEG OF LAMB

Charcoal: Indirect (pages 6-7)
Gas: Indirect/Medium Heat (pages 8-9)

  1 4- to 5-pound leg of lamb
  1 tablespoon dried parsley flakes
1½ teaspoons dried basil *or* oregano, crushed
  1 teaspoon salt
  ¼ teaspoon pepper
  1 cup water
  1 8-ounce can tomato sauce
  1 tablespoon lemon juice
  1 clove garlic, minced
  1 9-ounce package frozen artichoke hearts, separated
  ½ cup sliced pitted ripe olives
  ¼ cup crumbled feta cheese (1 ounce)

Remove fell (paper-thin, pinkish red layer) from outer surface of meat. Trim fat from meat. Combine parsley, basil, salt, and pepper; rub over lamb. Insert a meat thermometer near the center of the roast, not touching the bone. Place lamb in center of the cooking grill. Grill 1¼ hours or till meat thermometer registers 140°F (60°C). Remove lamb from grill. Transfer to an 11x7-inch roasting pan.

Combine water, tomato sauce, lemon juice, and garlic; pour over lamb. Toss together artichoke hearts and olives; arrange around lamb. Return lamb in roasting pan to cooking grill. Grill about 30 minutes more or till meat thermometer registers 160°F (71°C), basting occasionally with sauce, if desired.

Let roast stand 15 minutes before carving. Transfer roast to a serving platter. Using a slotted spoon, arrange artichoke mixture on serving platter with lamb. Drizzle with any remaining sauce. Pass feta cheese. Makes 10 servings.

Per Serving: 267 calories, 36 g. protein, 5 g. carbohydrate, 12 g. fat, 112 mg. cholesterol, 529 mg. sodium.

SKEWERED LEG OF LAMB

Charcoal: Indirect (pages 6-7)
Gas: Indirect/Medium Heat (pages 8-9)

 1 8-ounce jar (1 cup) Dijon-style mustard
 ½ cup cooking oil
 2 tablespoons dry red wine
 2 cloves garlic, minced
 1 teaspoon dried rosemary, crushed
 1 teaspoon dried basil, crushed
 ½ teaspoon dried oregano, crushed
 ½ teaspoon dried thyme, crushed
 ¼ teaspoon pepper
 1 4-pound leg of lamb, boned and
    butterflied

Combine mustard, oil, wine, garlic, rosemary, basil, oregano, thyme, and pepper.

Remove fell (paper-thin, pinkish red layer) from outer surface of meat. Trim fat. Place lamb in a shallow dish. Spread lamb with mustard mixture. Cover and marinate 4 hours or overnight in the refrigerator.

Drain lamb, reserving marinade. Thread two 12-inch skewers through meat, crisscrossing diagonally. Insert meat thermometer into thickest part of meat. Place lamb in center of the cooking grill. Grill 45 to 55 minutes for rare 140°F (60°C), 55 to 65 minutes for medium 160°F (71°C), or 1 to 1¼ hours for medium-well 170°F (77°C). Brush with reserved marinade during the last 10 minutes of grilling time. Makes 16 servings.

Note: This juicy lamb makes extraordinary sandwiches for a crowd. Split three 16-ounce loaves of French or sourdough bread lengthwise and spread softened margarine or butter on cut surfaces. Place bread, cut side down, on the outside edge of the grill for 1 to 2 minutes or just till lightly toasted. Slice lamb and place on bottom halves of bread. Replace tops and cut *each* loaf into 6 servings. If desired, serve with Yogurt-Cucumber Sauce (see recipe, page 111).

Per Serving: 230 calories, 25 g. protein, 6 g. carbohydrate, 16 g. fat, 68 mg. cholesterol, 518 mg. sodium.

HERB-COATED RACK OF LAMB

Charcoal: Indirect (pages 6-7)
Gas: Indirect/Medium Heat (pages 8-9)

 1 2½- to 3-pound lamb rib roast (8 ribs)
 1 tablespoon Dijon-style mustard
 1 cup soft bread crumbs
 ¼ cup snipped fresh parsley *or* 4 teaspoons
    dried parsley flakes
 2 tablespoons margarine *or* butter, melted
 1 clove garlic, minced

Trim fat from roast. Spread mustard over lamb; place, rib side up, in Weber® 13x9-inch aluminum pan. Combine bread crumbs, parsley, ¼ teaspoon *salt,* and ⅛ teaspoon *pepper.* Stir in margarine and garlic. Pat mixture on meaty side of roast. Place pan of lamb in center of cooking grill. Grill 1 to 1¼ hours for rare 140°F (60°C), 1¼ to 1½ hours for medium 160°F (71°C), or 1½ to 1¾ hour for medium-well 170°F (77°C). Let stand 15 minutes. Makes 4 servings.

Per Serving: 348 calories, 32 g. protein, 8 g. carbohydrate, 21 g. fat, 100 mg. cholesterol, 467 mg. sodium.

LAMB CHOPS WITH TANGY MUSTARD SAUCE

Charcoal: Direct (pages 6-7)
Gas: Indirect/Medium Heat (pages 8-9)

 ½ cup dairy sour cream
 3 to 4 teaspoons Dijon-style mustard
 1 clove garlic, minced
 8 lamb loin chops, cut 1 inch thick

Combine sour cream, mustard, and garlic. Trim fat from chops. Place chops on the cooking grill. Grill 7 to 9 minutes for rare 140°F (60°C), 10 to 13 minutes for medium 160°F (71°C), or 14 to 17 minutes for medium-well 170°F (77°C), turning once halfway through grilling time. Serve with sauce. Serves 4.

Note: Pictured on page 23.

Per Serving: 255 calories, 27 g. protein, 3 g. carbohydrate, 15 g. fat, 93 mg. cholesterol, 204 mg. sodium.

ORANGE-SPICED LAMB KABOBS

Charcoal: Direct (pages 6-7)
Gas: Indirect/Medium Heat (pages 8-9)

  1 pound boneless lamb round steaks *or*
      sirloin steak, cut 1 inch thick
 ⅓ cup olive *or* vegetable oil
 ¼ cup red wine vinegar
  4 teaspoons finely shredded orange peel
 ¼ cup orange juice
  1 green onion, thinly sliced
 ½ teaspoon ground cinnamon
 ¼ teaspoon ground cloves
  1 large zucchini, sliced ½ inch thick
 12 large fresh mushrooms
  4 cherry tomatoes

Cut lamb into 1-inch cubes; place in a plastic bag set into a shallow dish. For marinade, combine oil, vinegar, orange peel, orange juice, green onion, cinnamon, and cloves. Pour over lamb. Close bag. Marinate in refrigerator 4 hours or overnight, turning bag several times.

Drain lamb, reserving marinade. On four 12-inch skewers alternately thread meat, zucchini, and mushrooms. Place kabobs on the cooking grill. Grill 7 to 9 minutes for rare, 10 to 13 minutes for medium, or 14 to 17 minutes for medium-well, turning once halfway through grilling time. Brush with reserved marinade several times during grilling. Add cherry tomatoes to skewers during the last minute of grilling. Makes 4 servings.

Note: Serve rice pilaf as a tasty accompaniment.

Per Serving: 354 calories, 24 g. protein, 8 g. carbohydrate, 25 g. fat, 72 mg. cholesterol, 66 mg. sodium.

MARINATED MIXED GRILL

From the Weber® Grill Restaurant, Wheeling, Illinois

Charcoal: Direct (pages 6-7)
Gas: Indirect/Medium Heat (pages 8-9)

  4 lamb rib chops, cut ¾ inch thick
  6 ounces beef tenderloin cut into
      4 pieces
  6 ounces sweet *or* hot Italian sausage links,
      cut into 1-inch pieces
  1 whole medium chicken breast
      (¾ pound), split, skinned, boned, and
      cut into 1½- to 2-inch pieces
  4 ounces Canadian-style bacon, sliced
      ⅛ inch thick (8 slices)
 ½ cup olive oil
 ½ cup red wine vinegar
 ½ cup chopped onion
 ¼ cup snipped parsley
  2 tablespoons snipped cilantro *or* parsley
  1 teaspoon dried oregano, crushed
 ¼ teaspoon ground red pepper
 ¼ teaspoon salt
      Dash ground black pepper

Place lamb, beef, sausage, chicken, and Canadian-style bacon in a large plastic bag set into a shallow dish. For marinade, combine oil, vinegar, onion, parsley, cilantro, oregano, red pepper, salt, and black pepper; pour over meat in bag. Close bag. Marinate in refrigerator 6 hours or overnight, turning bag occasionally to distribute the marinade.

Drain meat. On *each* of four 12-inch skewers, thread a piece of beef, then Canadian-style bacon folded in quarters, a sausage piece, a chicken piece (folded in half, if necessary), and a lamb chop, skewered diagonally. Repeat with another piece of Canadian-style bacon, chicken, and sausage. Place kabobs on the cooking grill.

Grill 13 to 15 minutes or till sausage juices run clear, turning once halfway through grilling time. Makes 4 servings.

Note: Pictured on the cover.

Per Serving: 410 calories, 37 g. protein, 2 g. carbohydrate, 27 g. fat, 114 mg. cholesterol, 665 mg. sodium.

A NEW ZEALAND FEAST

*Lamb with Spiced Tamarind Glaze

*Sherried Kumaras

Marinated Vegetables

*New Zealand-Style Shortcake

Rosé Wine or Lemonade

Lamb with Spiced Tamarind Glaze is the dazzling entrée from Down Under. New Zealanders call this presentation of a double lamb roast a Guard of Honor. Golden *Sherried Kumaras*—New Zealand sweet potatoes—cook alongside the meat. Grill *New Zealand-Style Shortcake* during dinner; serve it warm and dusted with powdered sugar.

*Recipe included

53

LAND OF MEAT EATERS

Since the days of the first settlers from England, sheep have been a mainstay of the New Zealand economy, and lamb the most important meat. It's not uncommon for a household to eat lamb every day, for family dinners and special occasions alike. A Christmas tradition is the so-called "colonial goose," a stuffed leg of lamb.

New Zealand also has borrowed from the Maori, the original Polynesian inhabitants of the islands, its own version of the Pacific pit barbecue feast.

Called a *haangi,* the barbecue starts with a shallow pit and a pile of firewood covered with large stones. After the fire has burned to embers and the stones are hot, meat or poultry, vegetables (such as potatoes, kumaras, pumpkin, corn), and fish or shellfish are layered over them. Water is splashed over the stones to make steam, and the food is covered with clean sacks and earth. About an hour and a half later the pit is uncovered and the feast is ready.

LAMB WITH SPICED TAMARIND GLAZE

Charcoal: Indirect (pages 6-7)
Gas: Indirect/Medium Heat (pages 8-9)

- ¼ cup sugar
- 1 tablespoon cornstarch
- ¼ teaspoon ground cloves
- ⅛ teaspoon ground ginger
- 4 teaspoons tamarind pulp concentrate
- ⅔ cup water
- 2 8-rib lamb rib roasts (about 2½ to 3 pounds each)
- 2 medium onions, quartered

For tamarind glaze, in a small saucepan combine sugar, cornstarch, cloves, and ginger. Stir in tamarind pulp concentrate. Gradually stir in water. Cook and stir till thickened and bubbly. Cook and stir 2 minutes more.

Cut fat off the tops of the ribs so 1 to 1½ inches of bones are exposed (or, ask your butcher to trim the fat). With meaty sides out, tilt roasts and cross ribs so they interlock. Insert a meat thermometer into meatiest portion of ribs.

Place lamb in center of the cooking grill. Grill 45 minutes. Brush with tamarind glaze. Grill 15 to 30 minutes more for rare 140°F (60°C), 30 to 45 minutes more for medium 160°F (71°C), or 45 to 60 minutes more for medium-well 170°F (77°C), brushing once with tamarind glaze.

Remove lamb from grill and brush again with tamarind glaze. Let stand 15 minutes.

Meanwhile, place onion pieces on the cooking grill. Grill 10 to 12 minutes or till crisp-tender. Arrange on a serving platter with lamb. Heat remaining tamarind glaze and serve with meat. Makes 8 servings.

Note: Look for tamarind pulp concentrate at oriental stores. If you can't find it, substitute orange juice for the tamarind pulp and water. Pictured on page 52.

Per Serving: 253 calories, 25 g. protein, 9 g. carbohydrate, 12 g. fat, 84 mg. cholesterol, 78 mg. sodium.

SHERRIED KUMARAS

Charcoal: Indirect (pages 6-7)
Gas: Indirect/Medium Heat (pages 8-9)

    4 medium kumaras *or* sweet potatoes
         (about 1 pound)
    2 tablespoons margarine *or* butter
    ¼ cup orange juice
    1 tablespoon dry sherry

Scrub kumaras; pat dry. Prick with a fork. Bake kumaras in a 425°F (218°C) oven 40 to 50 minutes or till tender. [Or, micro-cook kumaras on 100% power (high) 7 to 9 minutes or till tender.] Cool slightly. Halve *each* kumara lengthwise and carefully scoop out center, leaving a ¼-inch shell.

In a medium mixing bowl combine kumara and margarine. Beat till fluffy. Gradually beat in orange juice and sherry.

Place kumara shells in a Weber® 13x9-inch aluminum pan. Spoon the kumara mixture into the shells. Place pan in center of the cooking grill. Grill 25 to 30 minutes or till heated through. Makes 8 servings.

Note: Kumaras are a variety of sweet potato native to New Zealand. To grill uncooked kumaras, prick with a fork and wrap in a square of heavy foil. Grill 45 to 60 minutes or till tender. Pictured on page 53.

Per Serving: 90 calories, 1 g. protein, 15 g. carbohydrate, 3 g. fat, 0 mg. cholesterol, 40 mg. sodium.

NEW ZEALAND-STYLE SHORTCAKE

Charcoal: Indirect (pages 6-7)
Gas: Indirect/Medium Heat (pages 8-9)

    2 cups all-purpose flour
    ½ teaspoon finely shredded lemon peel
    ½ cup cold butter *or* margarine
    2 beaten egg yolks
    4 cups fresh *or* frozen blackberries *or*
         boysenberries, thawed
 1¼ cups sifted powdered sugar
    ½ teaspoon ground cinnamon

Combine flour, lemon peel, and ¼ teaspoon *salt*. Cut in butter till mixture resembles coarse crumbs. Make well in center. Combine yolks and ¼ cup *cold water*. Add to flour mixture. Using a fork, stir till dough begins to cling together. Divide in half. Shape *each* portion into ball and roll between waxed paper into a 9-inch square.

Place 1 pastry square in 9x9x2-inch baking pan. Top with berries. Combine the 1¼ cups powdered sugar and cinnamon; sprinkle over top. Top with remaining pastry. Place pan in center of cooking grill. Grill 35 to 40 minutes or till golden. Let stand for 20 minutes. Serve warm and dusted with additional powdered sugar. Serves 9.

Note: Pictured on page 53.

Per Serving: 291 calories, 4 g. protein, 43 g. carbohydrate, 12 g. fat, 75 mg. cholesterol, 148 mg. sodium.

PERFECT TIMING

One day before:
☐ **Precook and stuff kumaras; chill.**
☐ **Marinate vegetables.**
☐ **Chill wine.**

Before serving:
☐ **Fire up the grill.**
☐ **Remove kumaras from refrigerator.**
☐ **Prepare lamb; begin grilling.**
☐ **Place kumaras on grill after lamb has grilled 45 minutes.**

☐ **Prepare dessert.**
☐ **Remove lamb from grill; let stand.**
☐ **Begin grilling the dessert and onion wedges.**
☐ **Pour wine.**
☐ **Prepare lamb, marinated vegetables, and kumaras for serving and call guests to dinner.**
☐ **Finish grilling dessert while eating main course.**

Made with crunchy corn chips and topped with creamy guacamole, *Mexican Burgers* make perfect fare for a patio party.

MEXICAN BURGERS

Charcoal: Direct (pages 6-7)
Gas: Indirect/Medium Heat (pages 8-9)

  1 **medium very ripe avocado, seeded, peeled, and cut up**
  1 **small tomato, peeled, seeded, and chopped (⅓ cup)**
  1 **tablespoon chopped onion**
  1 **tablespoon lemon *or* lime juice**
  ¼ **teaspoon salt**
  ⅛ **teaspoon garlic powder**
     Dash bottled hot pepper sauce *or* ground red pepper
  ½ **cup crushed corn chips**
  ⅓ **cup milk**
  2 **tablespoons finely chopped onion**
  1 **teaspoon Worcestershire sauce**
  1 **pound lean ground beef**
  4 **tomato slices**
  4 **lettuce leaves**
  4 **hamburger buns, split and toasted**

In a medium mixing bowl mash avocado. Stir in tomato, the 1 tablespoon onion, the lemon juice, salt, garlic powder, and hot pepper sauce. Cover and chill in the refrigerator till serving time.

Meanwhile, in another medium mixing bowl combine crushed corn chips, milk, the 2 tablespoons onion, and Worcestershire sauce. Add meat; mix well. Shape the meat mixture into four ¾-inch-thick patties.

Arrange patties on the cooking grill. Grill 11 to 12 minutes or till well-done, turning once halfway through grilling time. Serve patties topped with tomato slices and guacamole on lettuce-lined buns. Makes 4 servings.

Note: Toast the buns right on the grill.

Per Serving: 508 calories, 28 g. protein, 36 g. carbohydrate, 30 g. fat, 76 mg. cholesterol, 564 mg. sodium.

STUFFED DELI BURGERS

Charcoal: Direct (pages 6-7)
Gas: Indirect/Medium Heat (pages 8-9)

  ¼ **cup sliced green onions**
  1 **teaspoon instant chicken bouillon granules**
  ⅛ **teaspoon pepper**
  1 **pound lean ground beef**
  4 **slices liverwurst, cut about ¼ inch thick**
  2 **teaspoons brown *or* horseradish mustard**
  4 **slices rye bread, toasted**
  1 **tablespoon brown *or* horseradish mustard**
  4 **dill pickle slices**

Combine onions, bouillon granules, and pepper. Add meat; mix well. Shape meat mixture into eight ¼-inch-thick patties, about 3¾ inches in diameter.

Place liverwurst slices on *four* of the patties. Spread *½ teaspoon* of the 2 teaspoons mustard on *each* of the liverwurst slices. Top with remaining patties. Press meat around edges to seal well.

Arrange patties on the cooking grill. Grill 9 to 10 minutes or till medium doneness, turning once halfway through grilling time. Serve burgers open-face on toasted bread with the 1 tablespoon mustard and dill pickle slices. Makes 4 servings.

Note: Dress up your burgers even more with an assortment of sliced cheeses, lettuce leaves, and/or tomato slices.

Per Serving: 369 calories, 26 g. protein, 15 g. carbohydrate, 23 g. fat, 102 mg. cholesterol, 652 mg. sodium.

GREEK-STYLE BURGERS

Charcoal: Direct (pages 6-7)
Gas: Indirect/Medium Heat (pages 8-9)

- ½ cup plain yogurt
- ¼ cup peeled, seeded, and chopped cucumber
- ¼ teaspoon dried dillweed
- ¼ teaspoon dried mint leaves, crushed
- 1 beaten egg
- 2 tablespoons plain yogurt
- ¼ cup fine dry bread crumbs
- ¼ cup chopped onion
- ½ teaspoon dried oregano, crushed
- ¼ teaspoon salt
- ⅛ teaspooon pepper
- 1 pound lean ground lamb *or* beef
- 2 large pita bread rounds, halved crosswise
- 1 cup shredded lettuce
- 1 small tomato, seeded and chopped
- ½ small red onion, sliced and separated into rings

For yogurt sauce, combine the ½ cup yogurt, the cucumber, dillweed, and mint leaves. Cover and refrigerate at least 1 hour for flavors to blend.

In a medium mixing bowl combine egg and the 2 tablespoons yogurt. Stir in bread crumbs, the chopped onion, oregano, salt, and pepper. Add meat; mix well. Shape meat mixture into four ¾-inch-thick patties.

Arrange patties on the cooking grill. Grill 11 to 12 minutes or till well-done, turning once halfway through grilling time.

Meanwhile, wrap pita bread rounds in foil and heat on the edge of the cooking grill just till warm. Place meat patties in warmed pita rounds. Add lettuce, tomato, and onion slices. Spoon yogurt sauce on top. Makes 4 servings.

Per Serving: 404 calories, 38 g. protein, 27 g. carbohydrate, 15 g. fat, 160 mg. cholesterol, 457 mg. sodium.

CHUTNEY-STUFFED TURKEY BURGERS

Charcoal: Direct (pages 6-7)
Gas: Indirect/Medium Heat (pages 8-9)

- 1 beaten egg
- ¼ cup fine dry bread crumbs
- 2 tablespoons thinly sliced green onion
- 1 pound ground raw turkey
- ½ cup shredded carrot
- ⅓ cup finely chopped chutney
- 1 tablespoon fine dry bread crumbs
- 4 hamburger buns, split and toasted

In a medium mixing bowl combine egg, the ¼ cup bread crumbs, and green onion. Add meat; mix well. Shape meat mixture into eight ¼-inch-thick patties, 4 inches in diameter.

For stuffing, in a small bowl combine carrot, chutney, and the 1 tablespoon bread crumbs. Spoon about *1 rounded tablespoon* of the stuffing mixture over *half* of the patties. Spread to within ½ inch of edges. Top with remaining patties. Press meat around edges to seal well.

Arrange patties on the cooking grill. Grill 11 to 12 minutes or till no pink remains, turning once halfway through grilling time. Serve on toasted buns. Makes 4 servings.

Chutney-Stuffed Pork Burgers: Prepare burgers as above, *except* substitute 1 pound *lean ground pork* for the turkey and stir ¼ teaspoon ground *sage* and ⅛ teaspoon *pepper* into meat mixture.

Per Serving: 446 calories, 29 g. protein, 47 g. carbohydrate, 15 g. fat, 125 mg. cholesterol, 665 mg. sodium.

FRENCH MEAT LOAF

Charcoal: Indirect (pages 6-7)
Gas: Indirect/Medium Heat (pages 8-9)

    2 beaten eggs
    1 cup finely chopped onion
    ¾ cup cottage cheese
    ½ cup shredded cheddar cheese (2 ounces)
    ½ cup fine dry bread crumbs
    ½ cup chopped green pepper
    ⅓ cup tomato sauce
    ¼ cup dry red wine
    1 teaspoon Dijon-style mustard
    ¾ teaspoon salt
    ¼ teaspoon pepper
    1 pound lean ground beef
    ½ pound lean ground pork
    ½ pound ground veal
    8 small cornichons *or* sweet pickles
    3 tablespoons Dijon-style mustard

In a large mixing bowl combine eggs, onion, cottage cheese, cheddar cheese, bread crumbs, green pepper, tomato sauce, wine, 1 teaspoon mustard, salt, and pepper. Add ground meats; mix well. Pat mixture evenly in a metal 9x5x3-inch loaf pan.

Place meat loaf in pan in center of the cooking grill. Grill 50 to 60 minutes or till meat thermometer inserted near center of loaf registers 170°F (77°C) and no pink remains. Drain meat loaf. Let stand 15 minutes. Drain again, if necessary, and invert onto a serving plate. Serve with cornichons and the 3 tablespoons mustard. Makes 8 servings.

Note: Cornichon (KOR ni shon) is a French term for a very small, prickly cucumber grown in the West Indies and Southern United States and commonly pickled.

Per Serving: 339 calories, 31 g. protein, 16 g. carbohydrate, 18 g. fat, 154 mg. cholesterol, 806 mg. sodium.

PINEAPPLE-GLAZED HAM LOAF

Charcoal: Indirect (pages 6-7)
Gas: Indirect/Medium Heat (pages 8-9)

    ¼ cup packed brown sugar
    ¼ teaspoon ground cinnamon
    ⅛ teaspoon ground cloves
    1 beaten egg
    ½ cup fine dry bread crumbs
    ½ cup chopped onion
    2 teaspoons prepared mustard
    ¼ teaspoon white pepper
    1 pound finely chopped *or* ground
       fully cooked ham
    1 pound ground pork
    1 8¼-ounce can pineapple slices, drained

Combine brown sugar, cinnamon, and cloves; set aside. In a medium mixing bowl combine egg, bread crumbs, onion, mustard, and pepper. Add ham and pork; mix well. Arrange 3 pineapple slices in bottom of a metal 9x5x3-inch loaf pan. Cut remaining slice into 4 pieces; place between whole slices in pan. Sprinkle pineapple with sugar mixture. Pat meat mixture evenly into pan.

Place the ham loaf in center of the cooking grill. Grill 50 to 60 minutes or till meat thermometer inserted near center of loaf registers 170°F (77°C). Drain loaf; invert onto a serving plate. Serves 8.

Per Serving: 280 calories, 30 g. protein, 18 g. carbohydrate, 9 g. fat, 106 mg. cholesterol, 807 mg. sodium.

WHEN WELL-DONE IS WISE

Well-done is not ordinarily in the vocabulary of the grilling connoisseur. But for safety's sake, the U.S.D.A. recommends grilling meat *mixtures,* such as the burgers and meat loaves on these pages, till well-done 170°F (77°C) or till no pink remains.

When checking the temperature of a meat loaf, wait till near the end of the grilling time before inserting the meat thermometer. Insert the thermometer near center of loaf.

**Featured in this section
(clockwise from left):**
*Ricotta Chicken, Grilled
Chicken Salad,* and *Turkey
Drumsticks.*

60

MOIST, DELICIOUS POULTRY

CHICKEN BREASTS

Charcoal: Indirect (pages 6-7)
Gas: Indirect/Medium Heat (pages 8-9)

  2 **whole large chicken breasts (2 pounds total), halved lengthwise**
  ¼ **teaspoon salt**
  ⅛ **teaspoon pepper**

Remove skin from chicken breasts, if desired. Rinse chicken and pat dry. Season with salt and pepper. Place, bone side down, in center of the cooking grill. Grill 40 to 50 minutes or till chicken is tender and no longer pink. Makes 4 servings.

Orange-Ginger Chicken: Prepare as above, *except* omit seasonings. In a small saucepan heat together ⅓ cup *orange marmalade,* 2 tablespoons *soy sauce,* ¼ teaspoon ground *ginger,* and ⅛ teaspoon *onion powder* till marmalade melts. Brush on chicken during the last 10 minutes of grilling time.

Spaghetti-Sauced Chicken: Prepare as above, *except* omit seasonings. Brush chicken with mixture of ½ cup *spaghetti sauce* and 1 tablespoon *Worcestershire sauce* during the last 10 minutes of grilling time. Just before serving, sprinkle chicken with ¼ cup shredded *mozzarella cheese.*

Tropical Chicken: Prepare as above, *except* omit seasonings. Brush chicken with mixture of ¼ cup smooth *pineapple sauce,* 2 tablespoons bottled *barbecue sauce,* 1 tablespoon *vinegar,* and ⅛ teaspoon *garlic powder* during the last 10 minutes of grilling time.

Per Serving: 335 calories, 51 g. protein, 0 g. carbohydrate, 13 g. fat, 144 mg. cholesterol, 253 mg. sodium.

CHICKEN HALVES AND PARTS

Charcoal: Indirect (pages 6-7)
Gas: Indirect/Medium Heat (pages 8-9)

  2 **1¼- to 1½-pound broiler-fryer chicken halves *or* 2 to 2½ pounds meaty chicken pieces (breasts, thighs, *or* drumsticks)**

Remove the skin from the chicken, if desired. Rinse chicken and pat dry. Sprinkle with salt and pepper, if desired.

Place chicken, bone side down, in center of the cooking grill. Grill till chicken is tender. (Allow 1 to 1¼ hours for chicken halves or 50 to 60 minutes for meaty chicken pieces.) Serves 6.

Per Serving: 180 calories, 27 g. protein, 0 g. carbohydrate, 7 g. fat, 84 mg. cholesterol, 81 mg. sodium.

CUTTING UP CHICKEN

Follow these steps when cutting up a whole or a partially cut-up bird.

Step 1: With a sharp knife, cut the skin between the body and one thigh. Pull the thigh out and down until the bone pops out of the hip joint. Cut through the broken hip joint as close to the backbone as possible. Repeat on other side.

Step 2: To separate the thigh from the drumstick, cut through skin at knee joint. Bend joint backward until thigh and drumstick touch. Cut through knee joint. Repeat on other leg.

Step 3: To remove a wing, cut through the skin on the inside of the wing at the joint. Pull the wing out and down until the joint breaks. Cut through the joint. Repeat on other side.

Step 4: To divide the body, turn the bird on one side and cut between the breast ribs and back ribs on each side. Bend the back in half to break it at the joint; cut through the broken joint. Cut off the tail, if desired.

Step 5: Divide the breast in half by cutting lengthwise along the breastbone.

SPIEDINI

Charcoal: Direct (pages 6-7)
Gas: Indirect/Medium Heat (pages 8-9)

6 slices bacon
1 whole large chicken breast (1 pound),
    skinned, boned, and halved lengthwise
½ pound sweet Italian sausage links
3 whole large chicken livers
6 fresh sage leaves *or* several dashes
    ground sage
6 large mushroom caps
2 tablespoons melted margarine *or* butter

In a skillet cook bacon just till it starts to brown
and is not crisp; drain well. Rinse chicken breasts
and pat dry. Cut each chicken breast half
crosswise into thirds. Cut the sausage into
6 pieces. Cut chicken livers in half.

Place *one* of the sage leaves or a *dash* of the
dried sage on *each* liver half. Wrap bacon
around *each* liver half. On *each* of six 12-inch
skewers thread a sausage piece, followed by a
chicken piece and a bacon-wrapped chicken
liver. Thread a mushroom cap onto end of *each*
kabob. Brush kabobs with margarine.

Place kabobs on the cooking grill. Grill 12 to
14 minutes or till meats are tender, turning once
halfway through grilling time. Makes 6 servings.

Note: *Spiedini* is an Italian word meaning
"skewered." Follow the Italian tradition and serve
these kabobs with a pasta side dish.

*Per Serving: 274 calories, 29 g. protein, 1 g.
carbohydrate, 16 g. fat, 191 mg. cholesterol,
416 mg. sodium.*

TANDOORI CHICKEN

Charcoal: Indirect (pages 6-7)
Gas: Indirect/Medium Heat (pages 8-9)

2½ pounds meaty chicken pieces (breasts,
    thighs, *or* drumsticks)
2 8-ounce cartons plain yogurt
1 tablespoon grated gingerroot
2 cloves garlic, minced
2 teaspoons paprika
1½ teaspoons ground cinnamon
1 teaspoon ground cumin
1 teaspoon ground coriander
½ teaspoon salt
½ teaspoon pepper
¼ teaspoon ground cloves
½ cup chopped chutney
1 medium cucumber, sliced

Rinse chicken and pat dry. Place chicken pieces
in a plastic bag set into a deep bowl.

For marinade, combine yogurt, gingerroot, garlic,
paprika, cinnamon, cumin, coriander, salt,
pepper, and cloves. Pour over chicken. Close
bag. Marinate in the refrigerator overnight, turning
bag occasionally.

Remove chicken from bag, reserving marinade.
Place chicken pieces, bone side down, in center
of the cooking grill. Grill 50 to 60 minutes or till
chicken is tender and juices run clear, brushing
with reserved marinade during the last
10 minutes of grilling time. Serve with chutney
and sliced cucumber. Makes 6 servings.

*Per Serving: 321 calories, 28 g. protein, 26 g.
carbohydrate, 11 g. fat, 81 mg. cholesterol,
523 mg. sodium.*

SESAME CHICKEN

Charcoal: Indirect (pages 6-7)
Gas: Indirect/Medium Heat (pages 8-9)

    2 pounds chicken thighs
    ¼ cup minced scallions
    2 tablespoons sesame seed
 1½ teaspoons sesame oil
    1 teaspoon grated gingerroot
    1 clove garlic, minced
    ¼ teaspoon salt
    ¼ teaspoon ground red pepper

Remove skin from chicken. Rinse chicken and pat dry.

In a medium mixing bowl combine minced scallions, the sesame seed, sesame oil, gingerroot, garlic, salt, and pepper. Pat the sesame mixture onto chicken thighs.

Place chicken, bone side down, in center of the cooking grill. Grill 50 to 60 minutes or till chicken is tender and juices run clear. Makes 6 servings.

Note: Sesame oil is a full-flavored oil used frequently in oriental cooking. Look for it in the ethnic section of your supermarket or in an oriental food shop.

Per Serving: 186 calories, 22 g. protein, 1 g. carbohydrate, 10 g. fat, 70 mg. cholesterol, 161 mg. sodium.

GRILLED CHICKEN SALAD

From the Weber® Grill Restaurant, Wheeling, Illinois

Charcoal: Direct (pages 6-7)
Gas: Indirect/Medium Heat (pages 8-9)

    ½ cup mayonnaise *or* salad dressing
    ¼ cup honey
    2 tablespoons lemon juice
    3 whole large chicken breasts (3 pounds total), skinned, boned, and halved lengthwise, *or* 1½ pounds skinless boneless chicken breasts
    3 medium apples, cubed
 1½ cups sliced celery
    ½ cup chopped walnuts
    ¼ teaspoon salt
    ⅛ teaspoon pepper
        Lettuce leaves

For dressing, in a small mixing bowl combine mayonnaise, honey, and lemon juice. Cover and refrigerate till serving time.

Rinse chicken and pat dry. Place chicken breasts on the cooking grill. Grill 10 to 12 minutes or till tender and no pink remains, turning once halfway through grilling time. Cool 20 minutes or till cool enough to handle.

Cut chicken into 1-inch pieces. In a large bowl toss together chicken pieces, apples, celery, walnuts, salt, and pepper. Stir in dressing. Serve in a lettuce-lined salad bowl. Makes 6 servings.

Note: Pictured on page 61.

Per Serving: 428 calories, 29 g. protein, 26 g. carbohydrate, 24 g. fat, 83 mg. cholesterol, 287 mg. sodium.

SWEET-AND-SOUR CHICKEN

Charcoal: Indirect (pages 6-7)
Gas: Indirect/Medium Heat (pages 8-9)

  1 2½- to 3-pound broiler-fryer chicken,
      cut up
  1 8-ounce can pineapple chunks
  ¼ cup chicken broth
  ¼ cup soy sauce
  2 tablespoons brown sugar
  2 tablespoons cider vinegar
  1 clove garlic, minced
1½ teaspoons grated gingerroot
  4 teaspoons cornstarch
  1 green pepper, cut into 1-inch squares
  1 tomato, peeled, seeded, and cut into
      1-inch pieces
10 to 12 green onions, sliced diagonally into
      1-inch pieces
  3 cups hot cooked rice

Rinse chicken and pat dry. Place chicken pieces in a plastic bag set into a deep bowl. Drain pineapple, reserving juice.

For marinade, combine pineapple juice, chicken broth, soy sauce, brown sugar, vinegar, garlic, and gingerroot. Pour over chicken. Close bag. Marinate in the refrigerator 2 hours, turning bag occasionally.

Drain chicken, reserving marinade. In a small saucepan combine reserved marinade and cornstarch. Cook and stir till thickened and bubbly. Set aside. In a Weber® 8x5¼-inch aluminum pan combine pepper, tomato, green onions, and pineapple chunks. Stir in the thickened marinade.

Place chicken pieces in center of the cooking grill. Place vegetable mixture in pan beside chicken on cooking grill. Grill 20 minutes. Turn chicken pieces over and stir the vegetable mixture. Grill about 30 minutes more or till chicken is tender and juices run clear.

Transfer chicken pieces to a warm serving platter. Spoon vegetables and sauce around chicken. Serve with hot cooked rice. Makes 6 servings.

Per Serving: 357 calories, 31 g. protein, 41 g. carbohydrate, 7 g. fat, 84 mg. cholesterol, 805 mg. sodium.

INDONESIAN PEANUT CHICKEN

Charcoal: Indirect (pages 6-7)
Gas: Indirect/Medium Heat (pages 8-9)

  2 tablespoons chopped onion
  1 clove garlic, minced
  1 teaspoon cooking oil
  ½ cup peanut butter
  4 teaspoons soy sauce
  1 teaspoon brown sugar
  ⅛ teaspoon ground ginger
  ⅛ teaspoon crushed red pepper
  ½ to 1 cup hot water
  2 to 2½ pounds meaty chicken pieces
      (breasts, thighs, *or* drumsticks)
  1 green onion, thinly sliced
  1 tablespoon snipped cilantro *or* parsley

For peanut sauce, in a small skillet cook onion and garlic in oil till tender. In a food processor bowl or blender container combine onion mixture, peanut butter, soy sauce, brown sugar, ginger, and pepper. Cover and process or blend till smooth, adding enough hot water to give sauce desired consistency.

Rinse chicken and pat dry. Place chicken, bone side down, in center of the cooking grill. Grill 50 to 60 minutes or till tender and juices run clear, brushing generously with the peanut sauce during the last 10 minutes of grilling time. Arrange chicken on serving platter; sprinkle with green onion and cilantro. Makes 6 servings.

Per Serving: 297 calories, 26 g. protein, 5 g. carbohydrate, 20 g. fat, 64 mg. cholesterol, 374 mg. sodium.

BRUSH UP ON BRUSH-ONS

When grilling chicken pieces that you will brush with a sauce, place the chicken on the cooking grill *bone side down.* That way, you will be brushing the sauce on the meaty side, where the flavor counts most.

Filled with an orange-
and-almond rice
stuffing and glazed
with apple jelly,
*Chicken with Orange
Pilaf* tastes as
marvelous as it looks.

WHOLE CHICKEN

Charcoal: Indirect (pages 6-7)
Gas: Indirect/Medium Heat (pages 8-9)

    1   2½- to 3-pound broiler-fryer chicken
    ¼   cup cooking oil
    ¾   teaspoon salt
    ¼   teaspoon pepper

Rinse chicken and pat dry. Skewer neck skin to back. Tie legs to tail. Twist wing tips under back. Brush chicken with cooking oil. Season with salt and pepper. Place chicken, breast side up, in center of the cooking grill. Grill 1 to 1¼ hours or till meat thermometer registers 180°F (82°C) and the drumsticks move easily in their sockets. Transfer chicken to a serving platter. Let stand 15 minutes before carving. Makes 6 servings.

Italian-Style Chicken: Prepare as above, *except* omit cooking oil and seasonings. Combine 3 tablespoons *lemon juice,* 2 tablespoons *olive oil,* and 1 teaspoon dried *Italian seasoning.* Brush mixture on chicken occasionally during grilling.

Per Serving: 233 calories, 23 g. protein, 0 g. carbohydrate, 15 g. fat, 72 mg. cholesterol, 335 mg. sodium.

POULTRY SAFETY POINTERS

For the best flavor and quality, practice these safety tips when preparing and serving poultry.
  • Never thaw poultry on the countertop or in the sink, because bacteria can develop on poultry at room temperature. Thaw it in your refrigerator.
  • Wash your hands, utensils, and work surfaces with hot, soapy water after handling raw poultry to prevent spreading bacteria to other foods.
  • Cut raw and cooked poultry on an acrylic cutting board instead of a wooden board; wooden boards are difficult to thoroughly wash.
  • Use separate dishes for raw and cooked poultry.
  • Never leave cooked poultry stand at room temperature more than 2 hours.

CHICKEN WITH ORANGE PILAF

Charcoal: Indirect (pages 6-7)
Gas: Indirect/Medium Heat (pages 8-9)

    1   medium orange
    2   cups chicken broth
    1   cup regular brown rice
    1   shallot *or* green onion, chopped
    ½   teaspoon ground ginger
    ¼   teaspoon pepper
    ½   cup toasted slivered almonds
    1   3- to 4-pound broiler-fryer chicken
    ¼   cup apple jelly

Finely shred enough orange peel to make *1 teaspoon;* set aside. Peel and section the orange over a small mixing bowl, reserving the juice; set sections and juice aside.

For stuffing, in a medium saucepan stir together reserved orange peel, the chicken broth, rice, shallot, ginger, and pepper. Bring mixture to boiling; reduce heat. Cover and simmer 35 minutes. Stir in the reserved orange sections and juice and the almonds.

Rinse chicken and pat dry. Season the body cavity with ¾ teaspoon *salt.* Spoon stuffing into the neck cavity. Skewer neck skin to back. Lightly spoon stuffing into the body cavity. Tie legs together with string. Twist wing tips under back.

Place any remaining stuffing in center of a double thickness of heavy foil. Bring up 2 opposite edges of foil and, leaving a little space for expansion of steam, tightly seal top, then each end. In a small saucepan combine apple jelly and 1 tablespoon *water.* Heat till jelly melts.

Place chicken, breast side up, in center of the cooking grill. Grill 1½ to 1¾ hours or till meat thermometer registers 180°F (82°C) and drumsticks move easily in their sockets. Center of stuffing should register 165°F (74°C.) During the last 20 to 25 minutes of grilling time, brush bird with jelly mixture and place packet of stuffing on cooking grill beside chicken to heat through. Let stand 15 minutes before carving. Serves 6.

Per Serving: 413 calories, 34 g. protein, 38 g. carbohydrate, 14 g. fat, 85 mg. cholesterol, 613 mg. sodium.

RICOTTA CHICKEN

Charcoal: Indirect (pages 6-7)
Gas: Indirect/Medium Heat (pages 8-9)

- 1 2½- to 3-pound broiler-fryer chicken
- 1 cup ricotta cheese (8 ounces)
- ¼ cup grated Parmesan cheese
- 1 egg yolk
- 2 tablespoons snipped fresh parsley
- 2¾ teaspoons snipped fresh basil
- 1½ teaspoons snipped fresh tarragon
- 1 clove garlic, minced
- 2 teaspoons olive *or* vegetable oil
   Paprika

Rinse chicken; pat dry. With poultry shears, cut along both sides of backbone the entire length of chicken. Remove whole backbone and tail. Skewer neck skin to back. Twist wing tips under back. Or, if desired, cut off wing tips and discard. Place chicken, breast side up, on counter; press down on chicken to pop bones. Loosen chicken skin (see tip at right).

For stuffing, combine ricotta and Parmesan cheese, egg yolk, parsley, *2 teaspoons* of basil, *¾ teaspoon* of tarragon, and the garlic. Carefully spoon stuffing under skin (see tip at right). Make two 1-inch slits in skin on *each* side of bird, halfway between thigh and breast and about 1-inch from edge near tail end. (The slits should be parallel to the breast.) Push end of *each* drumstick through nearest slit to hold in place.

Brush chicken with oil. Sprinkle with remaining basil and tarragon and paprika.

For charcoal grilling, place chicken, breast side up, in center of cooking grill. For gas grilling, place chicken on rack in a Weber® 13x9-inch aluminum pan; place pan in center of cooking grill. Grill 1 to 1¼ hours or till meat thermometer registers 180°F (82°C). Let stand 15 minutes. To carve, cut gently through skin and stuffing down center of breast. Split *each* half by slicing between the thighs and breasts. Makes 4 servings.

Note: Pictured on page 60.

Per Serving: 419 calories, 41 g. protein, 5 g. carbohydrate, 25 g. fat, 176 mg. cholesterol, 267 mg. sodium.

HERB- AND LEMON-FLAVORED CHICKEN

Charcoal: Indirect (pages 6-7)
Gas: Indirect/Medium Heat (pages 8-9)

- 1 2½- to 3-pound broiler-fryer chicken
- 1 small lemon, cut into 8 wedges
- ½ teaspoon dried basil *or* tarragon, crushed

Rinse chicken and pat dry. Skewer neck skin to back. Twist wing tips under back. Lightly season chicken cavity with ⅛ teaspoon *salt*. Rub surface of chicken with *two* of the lemon wedges; place remaining wedges inside cavity. Tie legs with string. Sprinkle chicken with basil.

Place chicken, breast side up, in center of the cooking grill. Grill 1 to 1¼ hours or till meat thermometer registers 180°F (82°C) and drumsticks move easily in their sockets. Transfer chicken to serving platter; remove lemon wedges. Let stand 15 minutes before carving. Serves 6.

Per Serving: 156 calories, 23 g. protein, 1 g. carbohydrate, 6 g. fat, 72 mg. cholesterol, 113 mg. sodium.

STUFFING RICOTTA CHICKEN

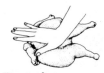

fingers. Be careful not to tear or cut the skin.

Press down on chicken with palms of hands to pop bones so the chicken will lie flat.

Carefully spoon stuffing under skin, pressing with fingers to distribute stuffing evenly over the legs, the thighs, and, lastly, the breast.

Starting at neck, loosen skin over breast, thighs, and legs with your

SHRIMP- AND CRAB-STUFFED CHICKEN WITH SEAFOOD SAUCE

Charcoal: Indirect (pages 6-7)
Gas: Indirect/Medium Heat (pages 8-9)

¼ pound fresh mushrooms, chopped
¼ cup finely chopped green onions
2 tablespoons margarine *or* butter
½ of a 4-ounce can small shrimp
1 cup cooked crabmeat, flaked
¼ cup crushed saltine cracker crumbs
   (7 crackers)
¼ cup dry white wine
2 tablespoons snipped fresh parsley *or*
   2 teaspoons dried parsley flakes
4 whole medium chicken breasts (3 pounds
   total), skinned, boned, and halved
   lengthwise
2 tablespoons dry white wine
4 cups hot cooked rice *or* fettuccine
   Seafood Sauce (see recipe below)

For stuffing, in a medium skillet cook mushrooms and green onions in margarine till tender. Remove from heat. Chop the shrimp and add to mushroom mixture. Stir in crabmeat, cracker crumbs, the ¼ cup wine, and the parsley; mix well. Rinse chicken and pat dry. Spoon about ¼ cup of the stuffing mixture onto *each* breast half. Roll chicken breast around stuffing and secure with wooden toothpicks.

Arrange stuffed breasts in a Weber 13x9-inch aluminum pan. Place pan in center of the cooking grill. Grill 35 to 40 minutes or till chicken is tender and no longer pink, basting once with the 2 tablespoons wine. Serve with rice and Seafood Sauce. Makes 8 servings.

Seafood Sauce: In a medium saucepan melt ¼ cup *margarine* or *butter*. Stir in 2 tablespoons *all-purpose flour*, ½ teaspoon *paprika*, and ¼ teaspoon *salt*. Add 1 cup *light cream* and 1 cup *milk*. Cook and stir over medium heat till thickened and bubbly. Cook and stir 2 minutes more. Stir in ½ cup cooked *crabmeat*, ½ of a 4-ounce can *small shrimp*, ¼ cup *dry sherry*, and 1 tablespoon diced *pimiento*. Heat through but do not boil.

Per Serving: 318 calories, 31 g. protein, 8 g. carbohydrate, 16 g. fat, 116 mg. cholesterol, 386 mg. sodium.

CHICKEN FAJITAS

Charcoal: Direct (pages 6-7)
Gas: Indirect/Medium Heat (pages 8-9)

3 whole medium chicken breasts
   (2¼ pounds total), skinned, boned, and
   halved lengthwise
½ cup vegetable oil
⅓ cup lime juice
¼ cup red wine vinegar
¼ cup chopped onion
2 cloves garlic, minced
1 teaspoon sugar
1 teaspoon dried oregano, crushed
½ teaspoon salt
½ teaspoon pepper
¼ teaspoon ground cumin
6 8- *or* 10-inch flour tortillas
1 medium avocado, seeded, peeled, and
   sliced
¾ cup chopped tomato
⅓ cup chopped onion
⅓ cup salsa

Rinse chicken and pat dry. Place chicken in a plastic bag set into a shallow dish. For marinade, combine oil, lime juice, vinegar, the ¼ cup onion, garlic, sugar, oregano, salt, pepper, and cumin. Pour over chicken. Close bag. Marinate in refrigerator 4 hours, turning bag occasionally to distribute marinade.

Drain chicken. Place chicken pieces on the cooking grill. Grill 10 to 12 minutes or till chicken is tender and no longer pink, turning once halfway through grilling time.

Meanwhile, wrap tortillas in heavy foil and place on side of the cooking grill. Grill about 5 minutes, turning foil packet over once.

Thinly slice chicken. Serve on warmed tortillas with avocado, tomato, the ⅓ cup onion, and salsa. Makes 6 servings.

Per Serving: 453 calories, 24 g. protein, 28 g. carbohydrate, 28 g. fat, 56 mg. cholesterol, 455 mg. sodium.

AN ITALIAN FEAST

*Antipasto Kabobs

*Roast Chicken with Tomato-Caper Sauce

*Zucchini-Cauliflower Toss

*Pepperoni Pizza Bread

Fruit-Flavored Gelato

Iced Coffee or Cappuccino

Savor *la dolce vita*—the sweet life—with an Italian-inspired dinner. Begin with quick *Antipasto Kabobs*, ready from the grill in two minutes. Then serve delicious Mediterranean-style *Roast Chicken with Tomato-Caper Sauce*, *Zucchini-Cauliflower Toss*, and *Pepperoni Pizza Bread*. *Buon appetito!*

*Recipe included

SEASONING GENIUS

Italian cooking is America's most popular ethnic cuisine. We're most familiar with the cooking of southern Italy, where meals are based on tubular pasta, tomato sauces, and olive oil. In the North, the pasta is ribbon shaped, the sauces are milder, and butter and cream are more often used.

Kitchens in both regions, however, are stocked with fresh or dried parsley, basil, marjoram, thyme, rosemary, sage, tarragon, bay leaves, oregano, and mint. Fennel seed, capers, and juniper berries also are favored. Spices include cloves, coriander, and saffron. Celery, onions, shallots, garlic, lemon juice, and olives complete the Italian spectrum of seasonings.

ROAST CHICKEN WITH TOMATO-CAPER SAUCE

Charcoal: Indirect (pages 6-7)
Gas: Indirect/Medium Heat (pages 8-9)

1 3½- to 4½-pound whole roasting chicken
1 lemon
2 tablespoons snipped fresh rosemary *or* 2 teaspoons dried rosemary, crushed
1 medium onion, chopped
2 cloves garlic
1 tablespoon olive *or* cooking oil
1 14½-ounce can peeled Italian-style tomatoes, cut up
½ cup tomato sauce
2 tablespoons dry white wine
1 tablespoon snipped fresh parsley *or* 1 teaspoon dried parsley flakes
2 teaspoons capers
⅛ teaspoon pepper
2 teaspoons cornstarch
1 tablespoon water
3 cups hot cooked pasta

Rinse chicken; pat dry. Sprinkle inside of cavity with ½ teaspoon *salt*. Squeeze juice of lemon inside and over skin of chicken; rub with rosemary. Skewer neck skin to back. Tie legs to tail; twist wing tips under back.

Place chicken, breast side up, in center of the cooking grill. Grill 1½ to 2 hours or till meat thermometer registers 180°F (82°C) and drumsticks move easily in their sockets. Let stand 15 minutes before carving.

Meanwhile, for tomato-caper sauce, in a saucepan cook onion and garlic in olive oil till onion is tender but not brown. Stir in *undrained* tomatoes, tomato sauce, wine, parsley, capers, and pepper. Bring to boiling; reduce heat. Simmer, covered, 5 minutes. Then simmer, uncovered, 15 minutes. Combine cornstarch and water. Stir into sauce. Cook till slightly thickened and bubbly. Cook 2 minutes more. Transfer chicken to a serving platter. Serve with pasta and tomato-caper sauce. Makes 6 servings.

Note: Pictured on page 70.

Per Serving: 417 calories, 38 g. protein, 29 g. carbohydrate, 16 g. fat, 104 mg. cholesterol, 523 mg. sodium.

ANTIPASTO KABOBS

Charcoal: Indirect (pages 6-7)
Gas: Indirect/Medium Heat (pages 8-9)

- 12 thin slices Genoa salami (3 inches in diameter)
- 24 cheese tortellini, cooked and drained
- 4 ounces Mozzarella cheese, cut into ¾-inch cubes
- ½ cup Italian salad dressing
- 1 16-ounce jar cherry peppers, drained
- 1 13¾-ounce jar marinated artichoke hearts, drained
- 12 green onions

Fold salami slices into quarters. On *each* of twelve 6-inch skewers thread 1 salami slice, 2 tortellini, and 1 cheese cube. Place in plastic bag; pour dressing atop. Cover; refrigerate several hours or overnight, turning several times. Drain. Transfer kabobs to Weber® 13x9-inch aluminum pan. Place pan in center of cooking grill. Grill 2 minutes or till cheese softens. Serve with peppers, artichoke hearts, and green onions. Serves 6.

Note: Pictured on page 71.

Per Serving: 429 calories, 19 g. protein, 24 g. carbohydrate, 32 g. fat, 62 mg. cholesterol, 1,203 mg. sodium.

ZUCCHINI-CAULIFLOWER TOSS

Charcoal: Indirect (pages 6-7)
Gas: Indirect/Medium Heat (pages 8-9)

- 1 small head cauliflower, broken into flowerets
- 2 medium zucchini, sliced ½ inch thick
- 2 tablespoons olive oil
- 2 cloves garlic, minced

Cut 18-inch square of heavy foil; place vegetables in center. Combine oil, garlic, ¼ teaspoon *salt,* and ¼ teaspoon *pepper;* drizzle atop. Bring up opposite edges of foil and, leaving a little space for expansion of steam, tightly seal top, then each end. Place in center of the cooking grill. Grill 35 minutes or till vegetables are tender. Serves 6.

Note: Pictured on page 71.

Per Serving: 59 calories, 1 g. protein, 4 g. carbohydrate, 5 g. fat, 0 mg. cholesterol, 6 mg. sodium.

PEPPERONI PIZZA BREAD

Charcoal: Indirect (pages 6-7)
Gas: Indirect/Medium Heat (pages 8-9)

- 2 to 2½ cups all-purpose flour
- 1 package quick-rise active dry yeast
- 2 teaspoons sugar
- ¾ cup warm water 120°F (49°C)
- 2 tablespoons margarine *or* butter, melted
- ¼ cup grated Parmesan cheese
- ¼ cup finely chopped pepperoni
- ¼ cup snipped oil-pack sun-dried tomatoes (optional)

Combine *1 cup* of the flour, the yeast, sugar and ½ teaspoon *salt.* Add water and margarine. Beat with electric mixer on low speed ½ minute, scraping bowl constantly. Beat on high speed 3 minutes. Using a spoon, stir in cheese, pepperoni, sun-dried tomatoes, and as much of the remaining flour as you can. Turn out onto lightly floured surface. Knead in enough of remaining flour to make a moderately stiff dough that is smooth and elastic. Cover; let rest 10 minutes.

Shape dough into a round 8 inches in diameter. Place in a greased 9-inch round foil or baking pan. Cover; let rise in a warm place 30 minutes. Place bread in center of cooking grill. Grill 25 to 30 minutes or till bread tests done. Serves 6.

Note: Pictured on page 70.

Per Serving: 173 calories, 5 g. protein, 21 g. carbohydrate, 8 g. fat, 5 mg. cholesterol, 402 mg. sodium.

PERFECT TIMING

One day before:
☐ Assemble kabobs; marinate overnight.

Before serving:
☐ Mix bread; let rise.
☐ Fire up the grill.
☐ Grill bread.
☐ Prepare and begin grilling chicken.
☐ Prepare vegetables; add to grill after chicken has grilled 1¼ hours.
☐ Prepare tomato sauce, pasta, and beverage.
☐ Remove chicken from grill; let stand. Grill kabobs.
☐ Prepare chicken, vegetables, bread, and kabobs for serving and call guests to dinner.

WHOLE TURKEY

Charcoal: Indirect (pages 6-7)
Gas: Indirect/Medium Heat (pages 8-9)

1   10- to 12-pound turkey
1   tablespoon cooking oil
½   teaspoon salt
¼   teaspoon pepper

Thaw turkey, if frozen (see tip at right). Remove neck and giblets. Rinse turkey on outside and inside neck and body cavities; pat dry. Pull the neck skin to the back and fasten with a skewer. Twist wings under back and tie legs and tail together securely, or tuck legs under band of skin. Brush outer surface of turkey with oil and lightly season inside and out with salt and pepper.

Insert meat thermometer into center of thickest part of a thigh, not touching the bone. Place turkey, breast side up, in center of the cooking grill. Grill 2 to 3 hours or till meat thermometer registers 180°F (82°C) and the drumsticks move easily in their sockets.

Remove turkey from cooking grill. Let stand 15 minutes before carving. Serves 12 to 14.

Note: You can bake your choice of stuffing in 2 Weber® 8x5¼-inch aluminum pans or in a double-thick heavy foil packet on the cooking grill beside the turkey during the last 20 to 30 minutes of grilling time.

Per Serving: 271 calories, 45 g. protein, 0 g. carbohydrate, 9 g. fat, 117 mg. cholesterol, 197 mg. sodium.

TURKEY WITH SOURDOUGH STUFFING

Charcoal: Indirect (pages 6-7)
Gas: Indirect/Medium Heat (pages 8-9)

1   10- to 12-pound turkey
½   pound bulk pork sausage
1   cup coarsely chopped onion
½   cup chopped sweet red *or* green pepper
5   cups cubed sourdough *or* French bread
½   cup raisins
⅓   cup slivered almonds, toasted
¼   teaspoon celery seed
1   to 1¼ cups chicken broth
1   tablespoon cooking oil

Thaw turkey, if frozen (see tip at right). For stuffing, in a large skillet cook sausage, onion, and pepper till sausage is no longer pink; drain fat. In a large mixing bowl stir together the meat mixture, bread cubes, raisins, almonds, and celery seed. Stir in enough chicken broth to make a moist stuffing. Transfer stuffing to 2 Weber 8x5¼-inch aluminum pans; cover with foil.

Remove neck and giblets from turkey. Rinse turkey and pat dry. Lightly brush turkey with oil. Insert a meat thermometer into center of thickest part of thigh, not touching the bone.

Place turkey, breast side up, in center of the cooking grill. Grill 2 to 3 hours or till meat thermometer registers 180°F (82°C) and the drumsticks move easily in their sockets.

Bake stuffing in pans on the cooking grill beside turkey during the last 15 to 20 minutes of grilling time. Remove turkey from grill. Let stand 15 minutes before carving. Serves 12 to 14.

Per Serving: 409 calories, 50 g. protein, 17 g. carbohydrate, 15 g. fat, 125 mg. cholesterol, 396 mg. sodium.

TURKEY BREAST

Charcoal: Indirect (pages 6-7)
Gas: Indirect/Medium Heat (pages 8-9)

  1 **3- to 3½-pound turkey breast half**
  2 **teaspoons cooking oil**
  ¼ **teaspoon salt**
  ⅛ **teaspoon pepper**

Rinse turkey and pat dry. Brush outer surface of turkey breast with oil and lightly season with salt and pepper. Insert a meat thermometer into the center of the thickest portion of turkey breast.

Place turkey breast half in center of the cooking grill. Grill 1½ to 2 hours or till meat thermometer registers 170°F (77°C). Makes 6 to 8 servings.

Per Serving: 311 calories, 43 g. protein, 0 g. carbohydrate, 14 g. fat, 115 mg. cholesterol, 183 mg. sodium.

THAWING FROZEN TURKEY

Always fully defrost a whole turkey or turkey parts before grilling.
   Place the turkey, in its original wrapping, on a tray in the refrigerator. Allow 24 hours of thawing time for every 5 pounds of turkey.
   For fast thawing, place the turkey, in its original wrapping, **in a sink or large bowl. Cover with *cold* water. Change the water often. Allow about ½ hour of thawing time per pound.**
   ***Never let turkey stand at room temperature to thaw.* Bacteria that cause food poisoning grow at these temperatures.**

ORANGE-GLAZED TURKEY BREAST

Charcoal: Indirect (pages 6-7)
Gas: Indirect/Medium Heat (pages 8-9)

  1 **10-ounce jar orange marmalade (about**
       1 cup)
  2 **tablespoons lemon juice**
  1 **teaspoon prepared mustard**
       Dash ground cloves
  1 **3- to 3½-pound fresh turkey breast half**
       Orange slices, halved (optional)

For orange glaze, in a small saucepan combine orange marmalade, lemon juice, mustard, and cloves. Cook and stir over low heat till the marmalade is melted. Set aside.

Rinse turkey and pat dry. Insert a meat thermometer into the center of the thickest portion of turkey breast.

Place turkey in center of the cooking grill. Grill 1½ to 2 hours or till thermometer registers 170°F (77°C), brushing turkey generously with orange glaze during the last 15 minutes of grilling.

Transfer turkey to a serving platter. Pass any remaining orange glaze. Garnish with orange slices, if desired. Makes 6 to 8 servings.

Per Serving: 423 calories, 43 g. protein, 32 g. carbohydrate, 13 g. fat, 115 mg. cholesterol, 105 mg. sodium.

The secret to the exciting flavor of *Jalapeño Turkey Breast* is just beneath its skin. Serve the turkey with a zesty pineapple salsa.

JALAPEÑO TURKEY BREAST

Charcoal: Indirect (pages 6-7)
Gas: Indirect/Medium Heat (pages 8-9)

2 tablespoons jalapeño *or* apple jelly
½ teaspoon salt
¼ teaspoon ground cumin
¼ teaspoon pepper
1 3- to 3½-pound fresh turkey breast half
½ teaspoon cooking oil
1 fresh pineapple
2 fresh apricots, pitted and chopped
1 sweet red pepper, seeded and chopped
¼ cup jalapeño *or* apple jelly

In a bowl stir together the 2 tablespoons jelly, the salt, cumin, and pepper.

Use a sharp knife to remove bone from turkey breast, keeping skin intact; discard bone. Rinse turkey; pat dry. To loosen turkey skin, slip your fingers under skin of turkey breast, pulling it away from meat, but leaving skin attached at one long edge. Spread jelly mixture over the meat under the skin. Replace skin over jelly mixture, securing skin with wooden toothpicks, if necessary. Insert a meat thermometer into the center of the thickest portion of turkey breast.

Place turkey breast, skin side up, in center of the cooking grill. Brush skin with oil. Grill 1½ to 2 hours or till meat thermometer registers 170°F (77°C).

Meanwhile, cut six ½-inch-thick slices off bottom of unpeeled pineapple. Halve slices; set aside. For salsa, peel, core, and chop remaining pineapple (should have 1½ cups). In a small bowl combine chopped pineapple, apricots, sweet pepper, and the ¼ cup jelly. Cover and set aside.

During the last 10 to 15 minutes of grilling time, place pineapple slices on side of the cooking grill; heat through. Slice turkey; serve with salsa and grilled pineapple. Makes 6 to 8 servings.

Note: You can substitute canned apricots for the fresh fruit.

Per Serving: 392 calories, 44 g. protein, 23 g. carbohydrate, 13 g. fat, 115 mg. cholesterol, 278 mg. sodium.

HAZELNUT-PESTO TURKEY BREAST

Charcoal: Indirect (pages 6-7)
Gas: Indirect/Medium Heat (pages 8-9)

¼ cup hazelnuts, toasted
1 egg yolk
1 cup lightly packed fresh spinach leaves
1 cup lightly packed fresh basil leaves
1 tablespoon hazelnut oil *or* cooking oil
1 clove garlic, minced
¼ cup grated Parmesan *or* Romano cheese
1 2½- to 3-pound fresh turkey breast half
2 teaspoons cooking oil

For pesto, in a food processor bowl process hazelnuts till very finely chopped. Add egg yolk, spinach, basil, hazelnut oil, and garlic. Process till smooth. If necessary, stop processor and scrape container sides. Stir in Parmesan cheese.

Rinse turkey and pat dry. To loosen turkey skin, slip your fingers under the skin of the turkey breast to loosen it from the meat, leaving skin attached at one long edge. Spread the pesto over the meat under the skin. Replace skin over pesto. Insert a meat thermometer into the center of the thickest portion of turkey breast. Brush turkey with cooking oil.

Place turkey breast, stuffed side up, in center of the cooking grill. Grill 1½ to 2 hours or till meat thermometer registers 170°F (77°C). If desired, serve with steamed carrots and zucchini. Makes 6 to 8 servings.

Note: To skip a step in the preparation of this recipe, buy prepared pesto. Then simply add the ground hazelnuts to the pesto.

Per Serving: 342 calories, 39 g. protein, 2 g. carbohydrate, 19 g. fat, 133 mg. cholesterol, 154 mg. sodium.

CRANBERRY-CURRANT TURKEY

Charcoal: Direct (pages 6-7)
Gas: Indirect/Medium Heat (pages 8-9)

    4 turkey breast tenderloin steaks *or* boned,
         skinless chicken breast halves
         (1 pound total)
    ¼ teaspoon salt
    ⅛ teaspoon pepper
    ½ cup cranberry-orange sauce
    ⅓ cup currant jelly
    2 tablespoons vinegar
    ⅛ teaspoon ground ginger
         Cooking oil

Rinse turkey and pat dry. Sprinkle with salt
and pepper.

For glaze, in a small saucepan combine
cranberry-orange sauce, currant jelly, vinegar, and
ginger. Cook and stir over low heat till jelly melts.
Remove from heat.

Lightly brush the cooking grill with oil. Place
turkey steaks on the cooking grill. Grill 10 to
15 minutes or till tender, turning once and
brushing often with glaze during the last
5 minutes of grilling time.

Transfer turkey steaks to a serving platter. Pass
remaining glaze with turkey. Makes 4 servings.

*Per Serving: 252 calories, 26 g. protein, 33 g.
carbohydrate, 2 g. fat, 71 mg. cholesterol,
194 mg. sodium.*

TURKEY DRUMSTICKS

Charcoal: Indirect (pages 6-7)
Gas: Indirect/Medium Heat (pages 8-9)

    ½ cup catsup *or* hot-style catsup
    3 tablespoons water
    2 tablespoons brown sugar
    1 tablespoon vinegar
    1 teaspoon Worcestershire sauce
    ¼ teaspoon crushed red pepper
    ¼ teaspoon ground cinnamon
    4 ¾-pound turkey drumsticks

For sauce, in a small saucepan combine catsup,
water, brown sugar, vinegar, Worcestershire
sauce, red pepper, and cinnamon. Cook and stir
till bubbly.

Rinse turkey drumsticks and pat dry. Place
drumsticks in center of the cooking grill.

Grill 1 to 1¼ hours or till tender and meat
thermometer registers 180°F (82°C), generously
brushing with sauce during the last 15 minutes of
grilling time. Heat any remaining sauce and pass
with turkey. Makes 4 servings.

Note: To determine the doneness of turkey
drumsticks, test with a meat thermometer near
the end of the grilling time. Insert the
thermometer bulb into the thickest part of the
drumstick so it does not touch the bone.
(Pictured on page 61.)

*Per Serving: 277 calories, 33 g. protein, 16 g.
carbohydrate, 8 g. fat, 96 mg. cholesterol,
462 mg. sodium.*

ORIENTAL DUCKLING

Charcoal: Indirect (pages 6-7)
Gas: Indirect/Medium Heat (pages 8-9)

- 1   4- to 5-pound domestic duckling, cut into quarters
- ⅓   cup soy sauce
- ¼   cup prepared mustard
- 1   tablespoon wine vinegar
- 1   clove garlic, minced
- ¼   teaspoon ground ginger

Thaw duckling, if frozen. For sauce, in a small mixing bowl combine soy sauce, mustard, wine vinegar, garlic, and ginger. Set aside.

Rinse duckling quarters and pat dry. Cut wing tips and excess fat from duck and discard. Pierce duck skin in several places with a fork.

Place duck quarters, skin side up, in center of the cooking grill. Grill 1¼ to 1½ hours or till a meat thermometer inserted into thickest part of thigh registers 180°F (82°C) and the juices run clear, brushing generously with the sauce several times during the last half of grilling. Serves 4 to 6.

Note: Save yourself some work. Ask your butcher to cut the duckling into quarters for you.

Per Serving: 408 calories, 24 g. protein, 3 g. carbohydrate, 33 g. fat, 95 mg. cholesterol, 1,623 mg. sodium.

WINE-BASTED CORNISH HENS

Charcoal: Indirect (pages 6-7)
Gas: Indirect/Medium Heat (pages 8-9)

- 4   1- to 1½-pound Cornish game hens
- ⅓   cup clear Italian *or* Dijon vinaigrette salad dressing
- 2   tablespoons dry white wine
- ¼   teaspoon salt
- ⅛   teaspoon pepper

Thaw Cornish game hens, if frozen. Combine salad dressing and wine; set aside.

Rinse hens and pat dry. Season with salt and pepper, if desired. Place hens, breast side up, in center of the cooking grill. Brush with salad dressing mixture. Grill 45 to 60 minutes or till tender and no longer pink, brushing once with salad dressing mixture. Makes 4 servings.

Per Serving: 665 calories, 84 g. protein, 2 g. carbohydrate, 37 g. fat, 181 mg. cholesterol, 228 mg. sodium.

SPECIALTY BIRDS: HOW MUCH TO BUY

When buying less familiar types of poultry, you may wonder how much to buy to make sure everyone receives an adequate serving.

For domestic duckling figure on ¾ to 1 pound of duckling per person. For Cornish game hens, consider the appetite of the people you are feeding. Half of a 1- to 1½-pound hen per person is adequate for most, but if you're facing hearty appetites (or if you buy smaller hens), purchase 1 hen per person.

Complement these golden *Five-Spice Game Hens* with steamed vegetables, such as pea pods, sweet peppers, and baby turnips.

FIVE-SPICE GAME HENS

Charcoal: Indirect (pages 6-7)
Gas: Indirect/Medium Heat (pages 8-9)

     2   1- to 1½-pound Cornish game hens
     ¼   cup thinly sliced green onions
     ¼   cup molasses
     1   tablespoon cooking oil
     1   tablespoon lemon juice
  1¼   teaspoons five-spice powder
     ¼   teaspoon garlic salt
     ⅛   teaspoon five-spice powder
     ⅛   teaspoon salt
     ⅛   teaspoon pepper
         Steamed vegetables (optional)

Thaw Cornish game hens, if frozen. For glaze, in a small bowl combine green onions, molasses, cooking oil, lemon juice, the 1¼ teaspoons five-spice powder, and garlic salt.

Rinse Cornish game hens and pat dry. Sprinkle hen cavities with additional five-spice powder, salt, and pepper. If desired, tie legs to tail.

Place birds, breast side up, in center of the cooking grill. Brush with some of the glaze. Grill 45 to 60 minutes or till tender and no longer pink. After 30 minutes of grilling, brush again with glaze and cut the string, if legs are tied to tail.

To serve, halve hens lengthwise. Brush birds with remaining glaze and arrange on a serving platter with steamed vegetables. Makes 2 servings.

Per Serving: 726 calories, 85 g. protein, 24 g. carbohydrate, 32 g. fat, 181 mg. cholesterol, 274 mg. sodium.

CORNISH HENS WITH MANDARIN ORANGE RICE

Charcoal: Indirect (pages 6-7)
Gas: Indirect/Medium Heat (pages 8-9)

     4   1¼-pound Cornish game hens
     2   tablespoons chopped celery
     1   tablespoon margarine *or* butter
     2   cups hot cooked rice
     1   11-ounce can mandarin orange sections,
           drained
     ¼   cup slivered almonds, toasted
     1   small green onion, thinly sliced
     2   tablespoons orange juice concentrate
     ¼   teaspoon salt
     1   tablespoon cooking oil
     ¼   teaspoon paprika
     ¼   cup orange marmalade

Thaw Cornish game hens, if frozen. For stuffing, in a medium skillet cook celery in margarine till tender. Remove from heat. Stir in rice, oranges, almonds, onion, orange juice concentrate, and salt. Set aside.

Rinse Cornish game hens and pat dry. Lightly stuff hens with rice mixture and tie legs with string. Lightly brush hens with oil; sprinkle with paprika. Wrap any remaining stuffing in double thickness of heavy foil.

Place hens, breast side up, in center of the cooking grill. Grill about 1 hour or till tender and no longer pink. Place foil packet of stuffing on cooking grill the last 30 minutes of grilling time. Baste hens with orange marmalade during the last 15 minutes of grilling time.

Transfer hens and extra stuffing to a serving platter. Makes 4 servings.

Per Serving: 902 calories, 89 g. protein, 56 g. carbohydrate, 36 g. fat, 181 mg. cholesterol, 176 mg. sodium.

A
CHINESE
CELEBRATION

*Steamed Buns with
Sherry Dipping Sauce

*Plum-Sauced Duckling

*Pea Pod-Pepper Rice

Tossed Green Salad

Fresh Fruit Platter

Iced Tea

Create a masterpiece
of a Chinese repast.
For the first course,
cook Steamed Buns
with Sherry Dipping
Sauce on the grill.
Follow with delectable
Plum-Sauced Duckling
in a garland of green
onion brushes. Colorful
Pea Pod-Pepper Rice
heats on the grill with
the duckling.

*Recipe included

THE WORTHY DUCKLING

Chinese festivals revolve around traditional foods. When a child is born, the father presents red-dyed eggs to friends and relatives. Birthday dinners include a bowl of noodles, symbol of long life. And during the Moon Festival, the 15th day of the eighth lunar month, it's traditional to serve duckling and moon cakes.

Grilled duckling is often prepared with two sauces: a highly seasoned sauce rubbed over the inside of the bird, and a basting sauce brushed over the skin as the duckling cooks. The crisp, golden skin is as much a delicacy as the moist meat.

In China, cooking over hot coals is no weekend or warm weather activity, but an everyday cooking method. Kitchens are small, and most do not have ovens, but are equipped with gas-heated woks and rice cookers.

PLUM-SAUCED DUCKLING

Charcoal: Indirect (pages 6-7)
Gas: Indirect/Medium Heat (pages 8-9)

- 1 12-ounce jar plum preserves
- 1 tablespoon brown sugar
- 2 tablespoons vinegar
- 2 tablespoons thinly sliced green onion
- ½ teaspoon crushed red pepper
- ½ teaspoon ground ginger
- 1 4- to 5-pound domestic duckling, thawed
  Green onion brushes (optional)

For the plum sauce, in a small saucepan combine plum preserves, brown sugar, vinegar, green onion, red pepper, and ginger. Bring to boiling, stirring constantly. Remove from heat; cool slightly. Cover and refrigerate several hours or overnight to blend seasonings.

Rinse duckling and pat dry. Remove any excess fat. Prick skin all over with a fork. Skewer neck skin to back. Tie legs to tail and twist wing tips under back.

Place duckling, breast side up, in center of the cooking grill. Grill 1¾ hours. Brush generously with plum sauce. Grill about 15 minutes more or till drumsticks move easily in their sockets and duckling juices run clear. Brush again with sauce. Let stand 15 minutes. Transfer to a serving platter. Garnish with green onion brushes, if desired. Reheat remaining plum sauce and pass. Serves 4.

Note: To make green onion brushes, see the tip "Easy, Elegant Garnishes" on page 29. Pictured on page 82.

Per Serving: 627 calories, 22 g. protein, 64 g. carbohydrate, 32 g. fat, 95 mg. cholesterol, 78 mg. sodium.

STEAMED BUNS WITH SHERRY DIPPING SAUCE

Charcoal: Indirect (pages 6-7)
Gas: Indirect/Medium Heat (pages 8-9)

  2   dried black mushrooms
  ¼   cup shredded cooked pork, beef, chicken, *or* turkey
  1   tablespoon honey-flavored barbecue sauce
  ⅛   teaspoon five-spice powder
  5   frozen unbaked dinner yeast rolls, thawed
  2   large cabbage *or* lettuce leaves

Soak mushrooms in warm water 20 minutes or till softened. Squeeze to drain well. Finely chop mushrooms, discarding stems. Combine the mushrooms, cooked meat, barbecue sauce, and five-spice powder.

Press *four* of the rolls into 3½-inch circles. Divide filling evenly among rolls. Moisten edges. Shape dough around filling, sealing bottom and forming a ball. Divide remaining roll into 8 equal pieces; roll *each* into a 7-inch rope. Twist 2 ropes together and place around center of *each* roll with ends tucked under roll. Repeat. Cover and let rest 10 minutes.

Rinse cabbage or lettuce leaves; place moist leaves in a Weber® 8x5¼-inch aluminum pan. Place rolls, seam side down, on leaves. Cover tightly with lightly greased foil. Place pan in center of cooking grill. Steam about 25 minutes or till buns spring back when touched. Immediately remove buns to a rack. Discard leaves. Serve buns warm with Sherry Dipping Sauce. Serves 4.

Sherry Dipping Sauce: In a small saucepan combine ¼ cup *chicken broth,* 2 tablespoons *soy sauce,* 1 tablespoon *dry sherry,* and ¼ teaspoon *sugar.* Bring to boiling, stirring till sugar dissolves. Remove from heat; cool slightly. Or, make ahead and chill overnight. Just before serving, reheat till just warm.

Note: Pictured on page 83.

Per Serving: 146 calories, 6 g. protein, 20 g. carbohydrate, 4 g. fat, 8 mg. cholesterol, 798 mg. sodium.

PEA POD-PEPPER RICE

Charcoal: Indirect (pages 6-7)
Gas: Indirect/Medium Heat (pages 8-9)

  2   cups cooked rice
  1   small red pepper, seeded and cut into 1-inch strips
  1   cup fresh pea pods, cut into thirds
  2   tablespoons dry sherry
  1   tablespoon soy sauce

In a medium mixing bowl combine rice, pepper, and pea pods. Combine sherry and soy sauce; toss with the rice mixture. Transfer to a Weber 8x5¼-inch aluminum pan. Cover with foil. Place pan in center of the cooking grill. Grill about 20 minutes or till heated through. Serves 4.

Note: Pictured on page 82.

Per Serving: 141 calories, 3 g. protein, 29 g. carbohydrate, 0 g. fat, 0 mg. cholesterol, 260 mg. sodium.

PERFECT TIMING

One day before:
☐ **Prepare plum sauce for duckling.**
☐ **Prepare dipping sauce for the steamed buns.**
☐ **Prepare iced tea.**

Before serving:
☐ **Thaw rolls; soak mushrooms for steamed buns.**
☐ **Fire up the grill.**
☐ **Prepare duckling; begin grilling.**
☐ **Prepare meat filling for buns.**
☐ **Fill buns and let rest.**
☐ **Prepare salad.**

☐ **Steam buns after duckling has grilled 1¼ hours.**
☐ **Prepare rice dish.**
☐ **Prepare fresh fruit platter.**
☐ **Remove buns from grill, brush duckling with sauce, and grill rice dish.**
☐ **Serve steamed buns with dipping sauce to dinner guests as appetizer.**
☐ **Remove duckling and rice from grill, prepare for serving, and call guests to dinner.**

Featured in this section
(clockwise from back left):
*Curry-Buttered Shrimp
Kabobs, Lobster Tails,* and
Lime-Seasoned Salmon.

SUCCULENT
FISH AND SEAFOOD

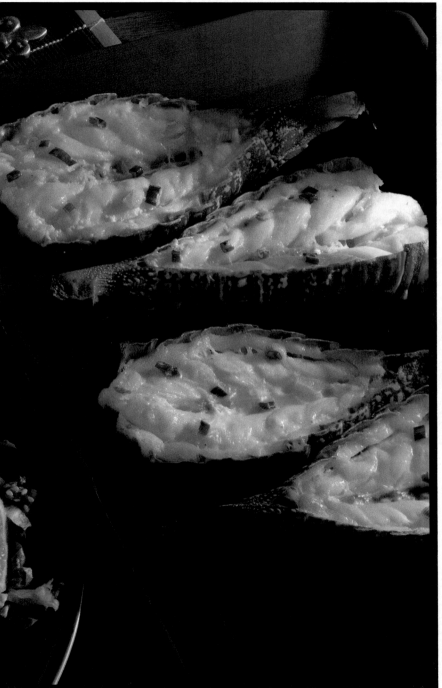

SWORDFISH STEAKS WITH RED PEPPER SAUCE

Charcoal: Direct (pages 6-7)
Gas: Indirect/Medium Heat (pages 8-9)

  4 fresh *or* frozen swordfish steaks, cut
       1 inch thick (about 2 pounds)
  2 tablespoons cooking oil
  ¼ teaspoon salt
  ⅛ teaspoon pepper
  1 recipe Red Pepper Sauce (see recipe,
       page 110)

Thaw fish, if frozen. Brush both sides of fish steaks with oil and sprinkle with salt and pepper. Lightly grease cooking grill. Place fish on the cooking grill. Grill 10 to 12 minutes or till fish flakes when tested with a fork, turning once halfway through grilling time. Prepare Red Pepper Sauce; heat in saucepan. Spoon over grilled fish. Makes 4 servings.

Per Serving: 368 calories, 40 g. protein, 4 g. carbohydrate, 22 g. fat, 78 mg. cholesterol, 458 mg. sodium.

HALIBUT EN BROCHETTE

Charcoal: Direct (pages 6-7)
Gas: Indirect/Medium Heat (pages 8-9)

1½ pounds fresh *or* frozen halibut steaks,
       cut 1 inch thick
  3 tablespoons cooking oil
  2 tablespoons lime juice
  4 teaspoons soy sauce
  ½ pound peeled and deveined large shrimp

Thaw fish, if frozen; remove skin and bones. Cut fish into 1-inch cubes. Combine oil, lime juice, and soy sauce; pour over fish. Let stand at room temperature 20 to 30 minutes. Drain fish; reserve marinade. Alternately thread fish and shrimp on four 12-inch skewers. Lightly grease cooking grill. Place skewers on cooking grill. Grill 10 to 12 minutes or till fish flakes; turn once and brush with marinade halfway through grilling. Serves 4.

Per Serving: 296 calories, 40 g. protein, 1 g. carbohydrate, 14 g. fat, 84 mg. cholesterol, 516 mg. sodium.

HERBED SALMON WITH MARINATED ONIONS

Charcoal: Direct (pages 6-7)
Gas: Indirect/Medium Heat (pages 8-9)

  4 fresh *or* frozen salmon steaks, cut 1 inch
       thick (about 1 pound)
  ¼ cup olive oil
  ¼ cup red wine vinegar
  1 tablespoon balsamic vinegar
       Dash pepper
  1 large red onion, thinly sliced and
       separated into rings
  1 tablespoon olive *or* cooking oil
       Dash salt
       Dash pepper
  4 small sprigs fresh rosemary *or*
       ½ teaspoon dried rosemary, crushed
  4 small sprigs fresh thyme *or*
       ½ teaspoon dried thyme, crushed

Thaw fish, if frozen. For marinade, combine the ¼ cup olive oil, red wine vinegar, balsamic vinegar, and dash pepper.

Place onion slices in a plastic bag set into a shallow dish. Pour marinade over onion slices. Close bag. Marinate 2 to 24 hours, turning bag occasionally to distribute marinade.

Brush salmon steaks with the 1 tablespoon olive oil; sprinkle with salt and dash pepper. Place 1 sprig *each* of rosemary and thyme on top of *each* salmon steak. (Or, combine the dried rosemary and thyme and rub ¼ teaspoon into *each* steak on both sides.) Cover and refrigerate salmon till ready to grill.

Lightly grease cooking grill. Place fish on the cooking grill. Grill 10 to 12 minutes or till fish flakes when tested with a fork, turning once halfway through grilling time. Remove onions from marinade with a slotted spoon; serve with salmon. Makes 4 servings.

Per Serving: 343 calories, 24 g. protein, 2 g. carbohydrate, 26 g. fat, 74 mg. cholesterol, 94 mg. sodium.

LIME-SEASONED SALMON

Charcoal: Direct (pages 6-7)
Gas: Indirect/Medium Heat (pages 8-9)

- 4 fresh *or* frozen salmon, whitefish, tuna, *or* sea bass steaks, cut 1 inch thick (about 1 pound)
- ¼ cup salad oil
- ¼ cup lime juice
- 1 tablespoon water
- 1 tablespoon soy sauce
- 2 teaspoons sesame oil
- 2 teaspoons honey
- 4 cups shredded mixed greens
- ½ cup shredded radishes
- ½ cup alfalfa sprouts
- 1 tablespoon toasted sesame seed
- 1 canned green chili pepper, rinsed, seeded, and chopped (optional)

Thaw fish, if frozen. Place the fish in a plastic bag set into a shallow dish.

For marinade, in a small mixing bowl combine salad oil, lime juice, water, soy sauce, sesame oil, and honey; pour over the fish. Close bag. Marinate in refrigerator 6 hours, turning bag occasionally to distribute marinade.

In a large mixing bowl toss together mixed greens, radishes, alfalfa sprouts, sesame seed, and, if desired, chili pepper. Transfer to a serving platter. Set aside.

Drain fish, reserving marinade. Transfer marinade to a Weber® 8x5¼-inch aluminum pan.

Lightly grease cooking grill. Place fish on the cooking grill. Grill 10 to 12 minutes or till fish flakes when tested with a fork, turning once halfway through grilling time. After turning, place pan of marinade on the cooking grill beside the fish. Grill marinade till bubbly.

To serve, pour hot marinade over greens on serving platter; toss to wilt slightly. Top with grilled fish. Makes 4 servings.

Note: Pictured on page 86.

Per Serving: 366 calories, 25 g. protein, 7 g. carbohydrate, 27 g. fat, 74 mg. cholesterol, 324 mg. sodium.

HALIBUT WITH FRESH HERBS

Charcoal: Direct (pages 6-7)
Gas: Indirect/Medium Heat (pages 8-9)

- 4 fresh *or* frozen halibut steaks, cut 1¼ inches thick (about 2 pounds)
- 2 tablespoons chopped fresh tarragon *or* 2 teaspoons dried tarragon, crushed
- 4 teaspoons snipped chives
- 2 tablespoons vegetable oil
- ½ teaspoon salt

Thaw fish, if frozen. Combine tarragon, chives, oil, and salt. Brush mixture onto both sides of halibut steaks. Arrange fish in a shallow pan. Cover; refrigerate 1 hour, turning occasionally.

Lightly grease cooking grill. Remove fish from pan and place on the cooking grill. Grill 10 to 12 minutes or till fish flakes when tested with a fork, turning once halfway through grilling time. Makes 4 servings.

Per Serving: 300 calories, 46 g. protein, 0 g. carbohydrate, 12 g. fat, 1 mg. cholesterol, 384 mg. sodium.

FISH-GRILLING KNOW-HOW

For easy removal of a tender, flaky fish from the cooking grill, try these simple suggestions.

Before grilling fish, lightly brush cooking oil or spray nonstick spray coating on the cooking grill. This helps prevent fish from sticking.

Turn fish only once, if necessary, and when you do, gently slip a wide spatula under the fish for the best support.

ITALIAN-STYLE FISH

Charcoal: Direct (pages 6-7)
Gas: Indirect/Medium Heat (pages 8-9)

 4 fresh *or* frozen halibut, salmon, shark, *or*
   swordfish steaks, cut 1 inch thick
   (1½ to 2 pounds)
 ¼ cup margarine *or* butter
 1 tablespoon snipped fresh basil *or*
   1 teaspoon dried basil, crushed
 2 teaspoons lemon juice

Thaw fish, if frozen. In a small mixing bowl combine margarine, basil, and lemon juice; beat till fluffy. Set aside.

Lightly grease cooking grill. Place fish steaks on the cooking grill. Grill 10 to 12 minutes or till fish flakes when tested with a fork, turning once halfway through grilling time.

Before serving, top *each* fish steak with a dollop of the margarine mixture. Serve immediately. Makes 4 servings.

Note: For accompaniments to this simple, yet elegant entrée, consider steamed fresh asparagus or zucchini, linguine with tomato sauce, a romaine and artichoke salad, and Parmesan-garlic Italian bread.

Per Serving: 282 calories, 34 g. protein, 1 g. carbohydrate, 15 g. fat, 0 mg. cholesterol, 222 mg. sodium.

SUMMER FISH STEAKS

Charcoal: Direct (pages 6-7)
Gas: Indirect/Medium Heat (pages 8-9)

 4 fresh *or* frozen halibut, salmon, *or*
   swordfish steaks, cut 1 inch thick
   (1½ to 2 pounds)
 ¼ teaspoon salt
 ⅛ teaspoon pepper
 2 tablespoons margarine *or* butter
 ½ cup chopped, seeded cucumber
 1 tablespoon snipped chives
 1½ teaspoons snipped fresh dill *or*
   ½ teaspoon dried dillweed
   Lemon wedges

Thaw fish, if frozen. Sprinkle both sides of fish steaks with salt and pepper.

Lightly grease cooking grill. Place fish steaks on the cooking grill. Grill 10 to 12 minutes or till fish flakes when tested with a fork, turning once halfway through grilling time.

While fish steaks are grilling, prepare cucumber-dill sauce. In a small saucepan melt margarine. Stir in chopped cucumber, chives, and dill. Heat through.

Arrange fish steaks on a serving platter. Drizzle the cucumber-dill sauce over fish. Serve with lemon wedges. Makes 4 servings.

Per Serving: 236 calories, 34 g. protein, 2 g. carbohydrate, 9 g. fat, 0 mg. cholesterol, 289 mg. sodium.

TUNA AND TABBOULEH PACKETS

Charcoal: Direct (pages 6-7)
Gas: Indirect/Medium Heat (pages 8-9)

  4 fresh *or* frozen tuna, halibut, *or* salmon
      steaks, cut 1 inch thick
      (1¼ to 1½ pounds)
  ¼ teaspoon salt
  ⅛ teaspoon pepper
  ¾ cup bulgur
  ½ of a small cucumber, chopped (½ cup)
  1 small tomato, chopped (½ cup)
  1 small carrot, shredded (½ cup)
  ½ of a small green pepper, chopped
      (⅓ cup)
  4 green onions, thinly sliced
  ¼ cup snipped parsley
  ¼ cup water
  ¼ cup olive oil *or* salad oil
  1 teaspoon dried rosemary, crushed
  ¼ teaspoon salt
  8 lemon slices

Thaw fish steaks, if frozen. Season fish with the ¼ teaspoon salt and the pepper.

For tabbouleh, in a large bowl combine the bulgur, cucumber, tomato, carrot, green pepper, onions, parsley, water, oil, rosemary, and the ¼ teaspoon salt.

Tear heavy foil into four 14x12-inch pieces. Spoon about ¾ *cup* of the bulgur mixture into center of *each* piece of foil. Top *each* with a fish steak.

Place 2 lemon slices on *each* fish steak. Bring up 2 opposite edges of foil and, leaving a little space for expansion of steam, tightly seal top, then each end.

Place foil packets on the cooking grill. Grill about 15 minutes or till fish flakes when tested with a fork, turning packets once halfway through grilling time. To serve, open packets and transfer fish and tabbouleh to serving plates. Makes 4 servings.

Per Serving: 409 calories, 38 g. protein, 30 g. carbohydrate, 16 g. fat, 64 mg. cholesterol, 330 mg. sodium.

PECAN-BUTTERED FISH FILLETS

Charcoal: Direct (pages 6-7)
Gas: Indirect/Medium Heat (pages 8-9)

  1 pound fresh *or* frozen fillets of sole,
      cod, turbot, whitefish, *or* haddock
  3 tablespoons butter *or* margarine
  ⅓ cup chopped pecans
  ¼ teaspoon salt
  ⅛ teaspoon pepper
  1 tablespoon snipped parsley
  ½ medium lemon, cut into wedges

Thaw fish, if frozen. For pecan butter, in a small saucepan melt butter. Stir in pecans. Cook and stir over medium heat about 3 minutes or till pecans are toasted and butter is dark brown. (Watch carefully because pecans can burn easily.) Set aside.

Cut large fillets into 4 equal portions. Pat dry. If fish fillets are ¼ to ½ inch thick, place skin side down in a lightly greased Weber® 13x9-inch aluminum pan. If fish fillets are ½ to 1 inch thick, place skin side down on the lightly greased cooking grill.

Grill 3 to 5 minutes for ¼- to ½-inch-thick fillets *or* 6 to 10 minutes for ½- to 1-inch-thick fillets or till fish flakes when tested with a fork. Halfway through grilling, turn the ½- to 1-inch-thick fillets.

Arrange grilled fish on a serving platter; season with salt and pepper. Spoon pecan butter over top. Sprinkle with parsley and serve with lemon wedges. Makes 4 servings.

Per Serving: 243 calories, 22 g. protein, 3 g. carbohydrate, 17 g. fat, 81 mg. cholesterol, 295 mg. sodium.

Fishermen have been grilling whole fish for centuries, but they never had specialties like *Whitefish with Garlic Butter* and *Rice-Stuffed Snapper.*

WHITEFISH WITH GARLIC BUTTER

Charcoal: Indirect (pages 6-7)
Gas: Indirect/Medium Heat (pages 8-9)

    1   2-pound fresh *or* frozen dressed
            whitefish, cod, pike, *or* red snapper
            (with head and tail)
    1   clove garlic, minced
    6   cloves garlic, halved
    2   green onions, thinly sliced
    ¼   cup butter *or* margarine
        Lemon wedges

Thaw fish, if frozen. Remove head and tail, if
desired. Rub the clove of minced garlic on inside
cavity of fish. Lightly grease cooking grill. Place
fish in center of the cooking grill. Grill 30 minutes
or till fish flakes when tested with a fork.

Meanwhile, for garlic butter, in a small saucepan
sauté halved cloves of garlic and green onions in
butter over low heat 12 to 15 minutes or till
tender and golden brown.

Arrange fish on a serving platter. Spoon garlic
butter over top. Serve with lemon wedges. Makes
4 servings.

Note: Cooking the garlic slowly in butter mellows
its sharpness and gives the garlic a sweet,
toasted flavor.

*Per Serving: 202 calories, 20 g. protein, 3 g.
carbohydrate, 12 g. fat, 78 mg. cholesterol,
164 mg. sodium.*

RICE-STUFFED SNAPPER

Charcoal: Indirect (pages 6-7)
Gas: Indirect/Medium Heat (pages 8-9)

    1   2-pound fresh *or* frozen dressed red
             snapper *or* redfish (with head and tail)
    ¼   cup wild rice
    1¼   cups chicken broth
    ¼   cup brown rice
    4   ounces mushrooms, sliced (1½ cups)
    2   tablespoons sliced green onion
    ½   cup chopped toasted pecans
    ½   teaspoon finely shredded lemon peel
    ¼   teaspoon pepper
    ¼   teaspoon salt
         Lemon wedges

Thaw fish, if frozen. Remove head and tail, if
desired. Rinse wild rice in a strainer under cold
water about 1 minute.

For stuffing, in a small saucepan combine wild
rice, chicken broth, and brown rice. Bring to
boiling; reduce heat. Cover and simmer
30 minutes. Add mushrooms and green onion.
Cook, covered, over medium-low heat 10 to
15 minutes or till vegetables and rice are tender,
stirring frequently. Stir in pecans, lemon peel,
and pepper.

Place fish in a Weber® 13x9-inch aluminum pan
or on a piece of heavy foil. Sprinkle cavity lightly
with salt. Spoon some of the *hot* rice stuffing into
fish cavity; press lightly to flatten evenly.

Spoon remaining rice stuffing on a piece of heavy
foil. Bring up 2 opposite edges of foil and, leaving
a little space for expansion of steam, tightly seal
top, then each end.

Place pan of fish in center of cooking grill. Grill
50 to 60 minutes or till fish flakes when tested
with a fork. Meat thermometer inserted in center
of fish stuffing should register 165°F (74°C).

Bake stuffing in foil packet on cooking grill beside
fish during the last 30 minutes of grilling time.
Use 2 large spatulas to transfer fish to a serving
platter. Serve with lemon wedges. Serves 4.

*Per Serving: 276 calories, 27 g. protein, 15 g.
carbohydrate, 12 g. fat, 40 mg. cholesterol,
426 mg. sodium.*

ORIENTAL GRILLED FISH

Charcoal: Indirect (pages 6-7)
Gas: Indirect/Medium Heat (pages 8-9)

  1 2-pound fresh *or* frozen dressed
        whitefish, lake trout, *or* pike
        (with head and tail)
  2 scallions, minced
  1 tablespoon grated gingerroot
  1 tablespoon soy sauce
  1 tablespoon sake *or* dry sherry
  1 tablespoon peanut oil *or* cooking oil
  ½ teaspoon sugar
  ½ teaspoon salt

Thaw fish, if frozen. Remove head and tail, if desired. Using a sharp knife, cut three ½-inch-deep diagonal slits, 1 inch apart, into both sides of fish.

For seasoning mixture, combine scallions, gingerroot, soy sauce, sake, oil, sugar, and salt. Rub fish cavity with some of the seasoning mixture. Rub remaining seasonings on outside of fish, pressing seasonings into the slits. Let stand at room temperature 30 minutes.

Lightly grease cooking grill. Place fish in center of the cooking grill. Grill about 30 minutes or till fish flakes when tested with a fork. Makes 4 servings.

Note: Scoring helps the fish absorb the blend of seasonings during grilling.

Per Serving: 154 calories, 19 g. protein, 2 g. carbohydrate, 8 g. fat, 97 mg. cholesterol, 582 mg. sodium.

CORN-BREAD-STUFFED TROUT

Charcoal: Indirect (pages 6-7)
Gas: Indirect/Medium Heat (pages 8-9)

  4 8- to 10-ounce fresh *or* frozen
        pan-dressed rainbow trout
  3 slices bacon
  ½ cup frozen whole kernel corn
  ½ cup chopped onion
  2 tablespoons canned chopped green
        chili peppers
1½ cups corn bread stuffing mix
  2 tablespoons margarine *or* butter, melted

Thaw fish, if frozen. In a skillet cook bacon till crisp. Drain bacon, reserving *1 tablespoon* drippings in skillet. Crumble bacon and set aside.

Cook corn and onion in the reserved bacon drippings over medium heat till onion is tender but not brown. Remove from heat. Stir in chilies, stuffing mix, and bacon. Toss lightly till well mixed. Add water as necessary to moisten (2 to 4 tablespoons), tossing gently to mix.

Place fish in a well-greased shallow baking pan or on a piece of heavy foil. To stuff fish, brush cavities with *half* of the margarine. Spoon the *hot* stuffing into *each* fish cavity. Press fish lightly to flatten evenly. Brush fish with the remaining margarine.

Place pan of fish in center of the cooking grill. Grill 12 to 15 minutes or till fish flakes when tested with a fork. Meat thermometer inserted in center of fish stuffing should register 165°F (74°C). Makes 4 servings.

Per Serving: 381 calories, 35 g. protein, 23 g. carbohydrate, 17 g. fat, 108 mg. cholesterol, 460 mg. sodium.

HORSERADISH-DILLED TROUT

Charcoal: Indirect (pages 6-7)
Gas: Indirect/Medium Heat (pages 8-9)

- 3 8- to 10-ounce fresh *or* frozen pan-dressed rainbow trout, lake perch, *or* pike
- ¼ cup whipping cream
- 2 tablespoons mayonnaise *or* salad dressing
- 1½ teaspoons snipped fresh dill *or* ½ teaspoon dried dillweed
- 1½ teaspoons prepared horseradish
- 6 sprigs fresh dill *or* ¾ teaspoon dried dillweed (optional)
- 2 tablespoons margarine *or* butter, melted
- ¼ teaspoon seasoned salt

Thaw fish, if frozen. For sauce, beat cream till soft peaks form. Fold in mayonnaise, snipped dill, and ½ *teaspoon* of the horseradish. Cover and chill up to 4 hours.

Spread inside cavities of the fish lightly with the remaining horseradish. Insert *two* of the dill sprigs into *each* fish cavity, if desired. (Or, sprinkle ¼ *teaspoon* of the dried dillweed into *each* cavity.)

In a small mixing bowl combine margarine and salt. Brush the fish with some of the margarine mixture. Lightly grease cooking grill. Place fish in center of the cooking grill. Grill 15 minutes or till fish flakes when tested with a fork, turning once and brushing with margarine mixture halfway through grilling time. Serve with sauce. Makes 3 servings.

Per Serving: 368 calories, 31 g. protein, 1 g. carbohydrate, 27 g. fat, 115 mg. cholesterol, 368 mg. sodium.

GRILLED CRUSTED TROUT

From the Weber® Grill Restaurant, Wheeling, Illinois

Charcoal: Indirect (pages 6-7)
Gas: Indirect/Medium Heat (pages 8-9)

- 4 8- to 10-ounce fresh *or* frozen pan-dressed trout
- 2 tablespoons olive oil
- ¾ cup fine dry bread crumbs
- ½ teaspoon garlic salt
- ¼ teaspoon paprika
- ¼ teaspoon white pepper
- ¼ teaspoon dried thyme, crushed
- ¼ teaspoon dried oregano, crushed

Thaw fish, if frozen. Remove heads, if desired. Split trout open like a butterfly. Brush both sides of trout with olive oil.

In a shallow dish combine bread crumbs, garlic salt, paprika, white pepper, thyme, and oregano. Place the fish in the crumb mixture, pressing lightly to coat both sides with crumbs.

Lightly grease the cooking grill. Place fish, flesh side down, in center of the cooking grill. Grill 8 to 10 minutes or till fish flakes when tested with a fork. Makes 4 servings.

Note: To avoid losing the crumb coating or breaking these delicate pieces of fish, grill the entire time on one side. No turning is necessary.

Per Serving: 299 calories, 32 g. protein, 14 g. carbohydrate, 13 g. fat, 84 mg. cholesterol, 310 mg. sodium.

A TASTE OF SCANDINAVIA

*Salmon with Horseradish Butter

*Creamed Winter Vegetables

Bread and Cheese Tray

*Pears in Lingonberry Sauce

White Wine and Coffee

Salmon is praised as Scandinavia's finest fish. Try *Salmon with Horseradish Butter* and you'll taste why. The easy, grilled accompaniments for the fish are *Creamed Winter Vegetables*—a rich-tasting medley of potatoes, carrots, and rutabaga—and irresistible cheese-filled *Pears in Lingonberry Sauce.* Enjoy!

*Recipe included

FRESH AND SIMPLE

Scandinavian waters are said to have 200 varieties of fish. They must be marketed fresh to satisfy choosy cooks, who prefer to buy fish live whenever possible. The Danes, in fact, use the expression "fresh as a fish" as we might say "fresh as a daisy."

For fish of such freshness and quality, no elaborate cooking or sauce is necessary. They're usually poached or grilled and served with a drizzle of butter, pepper, onion, and dill or cucumber.

Sport fishermen often provide fresh-caught salmon for the Midsummer's Day celebration in mid-June, the longest day of the year, when the sun skims the horizon but never sinks below it.

SALMON WITH HORSERADISH BUTTER

Charcoal: Indirect (pages 6-7)
Gas: Indirect/Medium Heat (pages 8-9)

- ½ cup butter *or* margarine
- 1 tablespoon prepared horseradish
- ½ teaspoon dry mustard
- ½ teaspoon snipped dill
- ¼ teaspoon salt
- ⅛ teaspoon white pepper
- 1 4- to 5-pound whole dressed salmon (head removed)
- 8 sprigs dill
- 1 small lemon, sliced
- 1 small red onion, sliced (optional)
  Additional lemon slices (optional)
  Additional sprigs dill (optional)

For horseradish butter, in a small mixing bowl beat butter 30 seconds to soften. Beat in horseradish, mustard, the ½ teaspoon dill, the salt, and pepper. Cover and chill butter till serving time.

Using heavy foil, fashion a foil pan to hold the salmon. Place sprigs of dill and lemon slices in cavity of salmon. Lay salmon in pan; place pan in center of the cooking grill.

Grill 45 to 60 minutes or till fish flakes easily when tested with a fork. Just before serving, skin salmon and transfer to a serving platter. Serve with horseradish butter. Garnish with sliced red onion, additional lemon slices, and additional dill sprigs, if desired. Makes 6 servings.

Note: Pictured on page 96.

Per Serving: 465 calories, 42 g. protein, 1 g. carbohydrate, 32 g. fat, 173 mg. cholesterol, 320 mg. sodium.

CREAMED WINTER VEGETABLES

Charcoal: Indirect (pages 6-7)
Gas: Indirect/Medium Heat (pages 8-9)

- 2 medium red potatoes, sliced
- 2 medium carrots, cut into thin strips
- 1 small rutabaga *or* 2 medium turnips, cut into thin strips
- 1 tablespoon margarine *or* butter
- 1 8-ounce carton whipping cream
- 1 tablespoon Dijon-style mustard
- ¼ teaspoon salt
- ⅛ teaspoon white pepper

In a large saucepan cook potatoes, carrots, and rutabaga in boiling salted water 5 to 10 minutes or till crisp-tender. Drain.

Cut an 18x12-inch piece of heavy foil. Transfer vegetable mixture to center of foil. Fold up foil around vegetables. Dot vegetables with margarine. Blend whipping cream into mustard; stir in salt and pepper. Pour over vegetables.

Bring up long edges of foil and, leaving a little space for expansion of steam, tightly seal top, then seal each end.

Place foil packet in center of the cooking grill. Grill 25 to 30 minutes or till vegetables are tender and cream is slightly thickened. Remove from grill. Open packet. Stir vegetables just before serving. Makes 6 servings.

Note: Pictured on pages 96-97.

Per Serving: 211 calories, 3 g. protein, 16 g. carbohydrate, 17 g. fat, 52 mg. cholesterol, 218 mg. sodium.

PEARS IN LINGONBERRY SAUCE

Charcoal: Indirect (pages 6-7)
Gas: Indirect/Medium Heat (pages 8-9)

- 6 small pears
- 1 3-ounce package cream cheese
- 1 tablespoon honey
- 2 tablespoons finely chopped almonds
- 1 14½-ounce jar lingonberries
- 2 tablespoons margarine *or* butter, melted
- ½ teaspoon ground cinnamon

Peel pears, if desired, working from the bottom. Remove cores from pears, leaving stems intact. Enlarge openings slightly. Beat cream cheese till fluffy. Beat in honey. Stir in almonds. Stuff cream cheese mixture into core areas of pears; set aside.

In an 8x8x2-inch baking pan combine lingonberries, margarine, and cinnamon. Place pears, filled side down, in lingonberry sauce. Cover pan with foil. Place in center of cooking grill. Grill 30 minutes or till pears are tender. Let stand 10 minutes before serving. Serves 6.

Note: You'll find lingonberries in the fruit, preserve, or gourmet section of your supermarket. Pictured on page 97.

Per Serving: 313 calories, 2 g. protein, 56 g. carbohydrate, 11 g. fat, 16 mg. cholesterol, 108 mg. sodium.

PERFECT TIMING

One day before:
- [ ] **Prepare horseradish butter and chill.**
- [ ] **Slice cheese for cheese tray.**
- [ ] **Chill wine.**

Before serving:
- [ ] **Fire up the grill.**
- [ ] **Prepare salmon and begin grilling.**
- [ ] **Prepare vegetable packet; begin grilling after salmon has grilled 30 minutes.**

- [ ] **Finish bread and cheese tray.**
- [ ] **Remove salmon and vegetables from grill; begin grilling the dessert.**
- [ ] **Pour wine.**
- [ ] **Prepare salmon and vegetables for serving and call guests to dinner.**
- [ ] **Continue grilling dessert and brew the coffee while eating the main course.**

Deviled Crab Lobster Tails combines the delicacies of lobster and crab with the cooking flavor of the grill.

LOBSTER TAILS

Charcoal: Direct (pages 6-7)
Gas: Indirect/Medium Heat (pages 8-9)

 4 7- to 8-ounce frozen lobster tails, thawed
¼ cup melted margarine *or* butter
 2 tablespoons dry white wine
 2 tablespoons thinly sliced green onion
    Dash bottled hot pepper sauce

Rinse lobster tails and pat dry. Use kitchen shears or a sharp, heavy knife to cut lengthwise through the centers of the hard top shells and lobster meat. Cut through the bottom shells and separate *each* half.

For brushing sauce, combine margarine, wine, green onion, and hot pepper sauce. Brush over the lobster meat.

Place lobster tails, shell side down, on the cooking grill. Grill 8 to 10 minutes or till meat is opaque. Pass remaining sauce with lobster tails. Makes 4 servings.

Note: For 5-ounce lobster tails, reduce grilling time to 5 to 6 minutes. For 10-ounce lobster tails, increase grilling time to about 12 minutes. Pictured on page 87.

Per Serving: 191 calories, 18 g. protein, 1 g. carbohydrate, 12 g. fat, 61 mg. cholesterol, 458 mg. sodium.

DEVILED CRAB LOBSTER TAILS

Charcoal: Indirect (pages 6-7)
Gas: Indirect/Medium Heat (pages 8-9)

 4 4- to 6-ounce frozen lobster tails, thawed
¼ teaspoon lemon-pepper seasoning
 2 tablespoons sliced green onion
 1 tablespoon sliced celery
 1 tablespoon margarine *or* butter
1½ teaspoons all-purpose flour
⅛ teaspoon dry mustard
¼ cup light cream *or* milk
½ teaspoon Worcestershire sauce
 1 6-ounce can crabmeat, drained, flaked, and cartilage removed
 2 tablespoons fine dry bread crumbs
 2 to 3 tablespoons margarine *or* butter

Rinse lobster tails and pat dry. Use kitchen shears or sharp, heavy knife to cut lengthwise through the centers of the hard top shells and lobster meat. Cut through the bottom shells and separate *each* half. Cut a lengthwise slit in the meat of *each* lobster tail half. Loosen the meat slightly, spreading the tail open. Do not remove meat from shells. Sprinkle slits with lemon-pepper seasoning. Set lobster tails aside.

In a small saucepan cook green onion and celery in the 1 tablespoon margarine till tender but not brown. Stir in flour and mustard. Add cream and Worcestershire sauce. Cook and stir till thickened and bubbly. Cook and stir 2 minutes more. Gently stir in crabmeat and bread crumbs.

Carefully spoon the hot crabmeat mixture into slits in lobster meat. Drizzle stuffed tails with the 2 to 3 tablespoons margarine.

Place stuffed tails, shell side down, in center of the cooking grill. Grill about 25 minutes or till lobster meat is opaque and stuffing is heated through. Makes 4 servings.

Per Serving: 198 calories, 19 g. protein, 5 g. carbohydrate, 11 g. fat, 73 mg. cholesterol, 495 mg. sodium.

CURRY-BUTTERED SHRIMP KABOBS

Charcoal: Direct (pages 6-7)
Gas: Indirect/Medium Heat (pages 8-9)

> 2   pounds fresh *or* frozen shrimp in shells
> ¼   cup butter *or* margarine
> 2   tablespoons finely chopped onion
> 1   to 1½ teaspoons curry powder
> 1   teaspoon snipped fresh dill *or*
>   ¼ teaspoon dried dillweed
>   Dash garlic powder
>   Fresh dill (optional)

Thaw shrimp, if frozen. For curry butter, in a small saucepan combine butter, onion, curry powder, dill, and garlic powder. Cook and stir over medium-low heat 2 minutes.

Peel and devein shrimp, leaving tails on. Thread shrimp on six 12-inch skewers, leaving space between pieces. Lightly grease the cooking grill. Place skewers of shrimp on the cooking grill. Brush with some of the curry butter. Grill 4 to 5 minutes or till shrimp turn pink, turning once and brushing with the curry butter halfway through grilling time.

Arrange shrimp kabobs on a serving platter. If desired, garnish with fresh dill. Makes 6 servings.

Note: Pictured on page 86.

Per Serving: 154 calories, 19 g. protein, 1 g. carbohydrate, 9 g. fat, 166 mg. cholesterol, 280 mg. sodium.

GRILLED SHRIMP WITH TOMATO RELISH

From the Weber® Grill Restaurant, Wheeling, Illinois

Charcoal: Direct (pages 6-7)
Gas: Indirect/Medium Heat (pages 8-9)

> 2   pounds fresh *or* frozen shrimp in shells
> 2   medium tomatoes, chopped
> ½   cup red wine vinegar
> ⅓   cup olive oil
> ¼   cup snipped parsley
> 2   tablespoons thinly sliced green onion
> 1   clove garlic, minced
> 1   tablespoon sugar
> ½   teaspoon salt
> ¼   teaspoon pepper
> 1   tablespoon olive oil
> ¼   teaspoon salt
> ⅛   teaspoon pepper

Thaw shrimp, if frozen. For tomato relish, combine tomatoes, red wine vinegar, the ⅓ cup olive oil, parsley, green onion, garlic, sugar, the ½ teaspoon salt, and ¼ teaspoon pepper. Cover and let stand at room temperature 5 to 6 hours.

Peel and devein shrimp, leaving tails on. Thread shrimp on six 12-inch skewers, leaving space between pieces. Brush with 1 tablespoon olive oil. Season with ¼ teaspoon salt and ⅛ teaspoon pepper.

Lightly grease the cooking grill. Place kabobs on the cooking grill. Grill 4 to 5 minutes or till shrimp turn pink, turning once halfway through grilling time. Serve with tomato relish. Serves 6.

Note: To give the shrimp a delicious smoked flavor, use mesquite wood in your charcoal or gas grill (see directions on page 12).

Per Serving: 230 calories, 19 g. protein, 5 g. carbohydrate, 15 g. fat, 166 mg. cholesterol, 468 mg. sodium.

FOIL-WRAPPED CLAM BAKE

Charcoal: Indirect (pages 6-7)
Gas: Indirect/Medium Heat (pages 8-9)

 4 4-ounce fresh *or* frozen lobster tails
 8 ounces fresh *or* frozen fish fillets, cut
    ½ inch thick
20 to 24 clams in shells
 4 ears of fresh corn
 1 bunch parsley
 ¼ cup melted butter *or* margarine
 1 medium lemon *or* lime, cut into wedges

Thaw lobster tails and fish, if frozen. Cut fish into 4 equal pieces; set aside.

Scrub clam shells under cold running water, using a stiff brush. In an 8-quart Dutch oven combine 4 quarts cold water and ⅓ cup *salt*. Add clams; soak 15 minutes. Drain and rinse clams, discarding water. Repeat soaking, draining, and rinsing twice more.

Husk corn and remove silk; break ears in half.

Cut four 18x18-inch pieces of heavy foil. For *each* packet, place *one-fourth* of the parsley in center of foil. Arrange the following on top of parsley: 5 or 6 clams in shells, 2 pieces of corn, 1 lobster tail, and 1 piece of fish. Bring up 2 opposite edges of foil and, leaving a little space for expansion of steam, tightly seal top, then each end.

Place foil packets, seam side up, in center of the cooking grill. Grill 25 to 30 minutes or till lobster is done and corn is tender. Discard any clams that do not open. Serve with butter and lemon or lime wedges. Makes 4 servings.

Per Serving: 317 calories, 28 g. protein, 23 g. carbohydrate, 14 g. fat, 105 mg. cholesterol, 360 mg. sodium.

MIXED SEAFOOD KABOBS

Charcoal: Direct (pages 6-7)
Gas: Indirect/Medium Heat (pages 8-9)

 1 8-ounce fresh *or* frozen lobster tail
 8 ounces fresh *or* frozen halibut fillets
    or steaks, cut ½ inch thick
 ¾ pound fresh *or* frozen shrimp in shells
 8 sea scallops
 8 medium mushroom caps
 ⅓ cup margarine *or* butter
 2 tablespoons lemon juice
    Lemon wedges (optional)

Thaw lobster, fish, and shrimp, if frozen. Remove shell from lobster; cut meat into 12 chunks. Cut halibut into 12 chunks, about the same size as the lobster chunks. Peel and devein shrimp. Rinse scallops and pat dry.

On six 12-inch skewers, alternately thread lobster chunks, halibut chunks, shrimp, scallops, and mushroom caps.

For lemon sauce, in a small saucepan melt margarine. Stir in lemon juice. Brush on kabobs. Lightly grease the cooking grill. Place kabobs on the cooking grill. Grill 8 to 10 minutes or till fish and seafood are opaque and cooked through, turning once and brushing with the lemon sauce halfway through grilling time. Pass additional lemon sauce. Serve with lemon wedges, if desired. Makes 6 servings.

Per Serving: 214 calories, 25 g. protein, 2 g. carbohydrate, 12 g. fat, 84 mg. cholesterol, 325 mg. sodium.

CARIBBEAN CUISINE

*Sofrito Shrimp

*Vegetable-Stuffed Chayotes

*Tropical Fruit Kabobs

Fruit Slush

Enjoy a taste of paradise without leaving your own patio. Grill *Sofrito Shrimp* atop the islands' traditional red beans and rice. A light touch of red pepper gives *Vegetable-Stuffed Chayotes* a taste of tropic heat. Then cool your taste buds with *Tropical Fruit Kabobs,* a sampling of lush Caribbean fruits brushed with a honey-lime sauce.

*Recipe included

105

ISLANDS OF THE SUN

Led by Columbus in 1492, wave after wave of Europeans discovered the beautiful islands of the Caribbean. Today the cooking is a rich ethnic stew of Dutch, French, Spanish, Portuguese, English, African, and Indian.

The Arawak Indians introduced newcomers to sweet potatoes, garlic, and corn and to a new cooking method.

They cooked meat, fish, and chicken on wood gratings over a hot fire and called it *barbacoa*—the original barbecue.

In Spanish-speaking parts of the Caribbean, foods are seasoned with sofrito, an aromatic and well-seasoned sauce of green peppers, onions, garlic, tomatoes, coriander, and annatto seed. Cooks make enough for a week at a time and add it to meat, fish, or poultry dishes or to rice.

SOFRITO SHRIMP

Charcoal: Indirect (pages 6-7)
Gas: Indirect/Medium Heat (pages 8-9)

- ⅔ cup long grain rice
- 6 slices bacon
- ½ cup chopped onion
- ½ cup chopped green pepper
- 2 cloves garlic, minced
- 2 large tomatoes, chopped
- 1 15½-ounce can small red beans, drained
- 2 tablespoons lime juice
- 2 pounds large shrimp, peeled and deveined (leave tails on, if desired)

In a medium saucepan bring 1⅓ cups *lightly salted water* to boiling. Add rice. Cover and simmer 15 minutes or till rice is tender and water is absorbed.

Meanwhile, in a large skillet cook bacon till crisp. Drain on paper towels, reserving *2 tablespoons* drippings in skillet. Crumble bacon and set aside. Cook onion, green pepper, and garlic in reserved bacon drippings till onion is tender.

Stir together cooked rice, crumbled bacon, onion mixture, tomatoes, beans, and lime juice.

Transfer rice mixture to a Weber® 13x9-inch aluminum pan. Arrange shrimp on top. Cover with foil and place in center of the cooking grill. Grill 25 to 30 minutes or till shrimp turn pink. Makes 6 servings.

Note: Pictured on page 104.

Per Serving: 308 calories, 26 g. protein, 31 g. carbohydrate, 9 g. fat, 199 mg. cholesterol, 573 mg. sodium.

VEGETABLE-STUFFED CHAYOTES

Charcoal: Indirect (pages 6-7)
Gas: Indirect/Medium Heat (pages 8-9)

    3 medium chayotes (7 to 8 ounces each),
         halved lengthwise
    ½ cup tomato sauce
    1 cup shredded spinach *or* Swiss chard
    ¼ cup chopped green pepper
    ¼ teaspoon salt
    ⅛ teaspoon ground red pepper

In a medium saucepan cook chayotes, covered, in boiling salted water 15 to 17 minutes or just till soft. Drain. Scoop out pulp, leaving ¼-inch-thick shells. Set shells aside.

Coarsely chop the chayote pulp. In a medium mixing bowl stir together the chopped chayote, tomato sauce, spinach, green pepper, salt, and red pepper.

Arrange the chayote shells in two Weber 8x5¼-inch aluminum pans. Spoon the chayote mixture into the shells.

Place the pans in center of the cooking grill. Grill about 20 minutes or till chayotes are heated through. Makes 6 servings.

Note: Pictured on page 105.

Per Serving: 33 calories, 1 g. protein, 7 g. carbohydrate, 0 g. fat, 0 mg. cholesterol, 224 mg. sodium.

TROPICAL FRUIT KABOBS

Charcoal: Indirect (pages 6-7)
Gas: Indirect/Medium Heat (pages 8-9)

    1 medium banana, peeled and sliced into
         1-inch pieces
    2 medium carambola (star fruit), sliced
         ½ inch thick
    1 small pineapple, cored, and cut into
         1-inch cubes
    ½ of a medium papaya, peeled, seeded,
         and cut into 1-inch cubes
    2 tablespoons honey
    2 tablespoons lime juice
       Dash curry powder

On six 12-inch skewers alternately thread banana, carambola, pineapple, and papaya, leaving space between pieces.

For sauce, combine honey, lime juice, and curry powder. Place kabobs in center of the cooking grill. Grill 3 minutes. Brush with some of the sauce and grill about 5 minutes more or till heated through. Just before serving, brush kabobs with remaining sauce. Makes 6 servings.

Note: Pictured on pages 104-105.

Per Serving: 86 calories, 1 g. protein, 22 g. carbohydrate, 0 g. fat, 0 mg. cholesterol, 3 mg. sodium.

PERFECT TIMING

One day before:
☐ **Precook and stuff chayotes; cover and refrigerate.**
☐ **Prepare fruit slush and freeze.**
☐ **Peel and devein shrimp; cover and refrigerate.**

Before serving:
☐ **Remove chayotes from refrigerator and slush from freezer; let stand at room temperature.**
☐ **Fire up the grill.**

☐ **Prepare shrimp entrée and begin grilling. Add stuffed chayotes to grill.**
☐ **Prepare the fruit kabobs.**
☐ **Remove shrimp and chayotes from the grill.**
☐ **Serve fruit slush.**
☐ **Prepare shrimp and chayotes for serving and call guests to dinner**
☐ **Grill fruit kabobs while eating the main course.**

Featured in this section (from left to right): *Yogurt-Cucumber Sauce, Cajun Salsa, Mustard Sauce,* and *Korean Marinade.*

MIX-AND-MATCH SAUCES AND MARINADES

TOMATILLO SAUCE

 8 to 10 fresh tomatillos *or* one 18-ounce
   can tomatillos, drained
 1 or 2 jalapeño peppers, seeded and
   finely chopped
 2 tablespoons finely chopped onion
 1 clove garlic, minced
 1 teaspoon snipped cilantro *or* parsley
 ⅛ teaspoon sugar

Remove outer leaves of fresh tomatillos. Place on
baking sheet. Bake in 425°F (218°C) oven about
20 minutes or till blisters form. Cool. Remove and
discard stem end of tomatillos and finely chop.
Or, rinse and finely chop canned tomatillos.

In a small mixing bowl combine tomatillos,
peppers, onion, garlic, cilantro, and sugar. If using
fresh tomatillos, add ¼ teaspoon *salt*. Cover and
refrigerate several hours or overnight, stirring
occasionally. Serve with grilled chicken or pork.
Makes 1 cup (sixteen 1-tablespoon servings).

Note: Tomatillos are Mexican green tomatoes.

*Per Serving: 7 calories, 0 g. protein, 1 g.
carbohydrate, 0 g. fat, 0 mg. cholesterol,
70 mg. sodium.*

MUSTARD SAUCE

 3 tablespoons water
 2 tablespoons dry mustard
 1 teaspoon cornstarch
 3 tablespoons light corn syrup
 1 tablespoon vinegar
 ¼ teaspoon dried tarragon *or* basil, crushed

In saucepan combine water, mustard, and
cornstarch. Stir in syrup, vinegar, and tarragon.
Cook and stir till thickened and bubbly. Cook and
stir 2 minutes more. Brush onto sausages, burgers,
or pork during the last 10 minutes of grilling time.
Cover and refrigerate up to 2 weeks. Makes
⅓ cup (five 1-tablespoon servings).

Note: Pictured on page 109.

*Per Serving: 55 calories, 0 g. protein, 10 g.
carbohydrate, 0 g. fat, 0 mg. cholesterol,
6 mg. sodium.*

HERB-BUTTER SAUCE

 ½ cup butter *or* margarine
 4 teaspoons snipped fresh basil *or*
   1½ teaspoons dried basil, crushed
 1½ teaspoons snipped fresh oregano *or*
   ½ teaspoon dried oregano, crushed
 1½ teaspoons snipped fresh tarragon *or*
   ½ teaspoon dried tarragon, crushed
 ½ teaspoon snipped chives
 ½ teaspoon snipped fresh thyme *or* dash
   dried thyme, crushed
   Dash pepper

In a saucepan melt butter. Stir in remaining
ingredients. Cook 1 to 2 minutes to blend flavors.
Serve with grilled fish or vegetables. Makes about
½ cup (eight 1-tablespoon servings).

*Per Serving: 103 calories, 0 g. protein, 0 g.
carbohydrate, 12 g. fat, 31 mg. cholesterol,
97 mg. sodium.*

RED PEPPER SAUCE

 1 large sweet red pepper, roasted, peeled,
   and seeded, *or* ½ cup canned roasted
   red peppers
 4 green onions, sliced
 1 clove garlic, halved
 2 tablespoons cooking oil
 2 teaspoons Dijon-style mustard
 1 teaspoon honey
 ¾ cup snipped fresh basil *or* ¼ teaspoon
   dried basil, crushed
 ⅛ teaspoon salt
   Dash black pepper

Coarsely chop red pepper; set aside. In a skillet
cook onions and garlic in oil till tender. Remove
from heat; cool slightly. In blender container or
food processor bowl combine red pepper, onion
mixture, mustard, honey, basil, salt, and black
pepper. Cover; blend or process till smooth.

Serve warm over grilled fish, chicken, or pork.
Store, covered, in refrigerator up to 1 week.
Makes ½ cup (eight 1-tablespoon servings).

*Per Serving: 38 calories, 0 g. protein, 2 g.
carbohydrate, 4 g. fat, 0 mg. cholesterol,
73 mg. sodium.*

YOGURT-CUCUMBER SAUCE

 1 **small tomato, peeled and seeded**
 ½ **of a cucumber, peeled**
 ½ **cup plain yogurt**
 1 **tablespoon finely chopped onion**
 1 **small clove garlic, minced**
 1 **tablespoon snipped fresh parsley** *or*
    1 **teaspoon dried parsley flakes**
 ½ **teaspoon snipped fresh mint** *or*
    ⅛ **teaspoon dried mint leaves, crushed**
 ⅛ **teaspoon salt**

Finely chop tomato; drain well. Slice cucumber in half lengthwise; scoop out seeds and discard. Shred cucumber; drain well.

In a small bowl stir together yogurt, onion, garlic, parsley, mint, and salt. Stir in tomato and cucumber. Chill 1 hour. Serve with grilled lamb. Makes 1 cup (eight 2-tablespoon servings).

Note: Pictured on page 112.

Per Serving: 15 calories, 1 g. protein, 2 g. carbohydrate, 0 g. fat, 1 mg. cholesterol, 45 mg. sodium.

ORIENTAL SAUCE

 ½ **cup hoisin sauce**
 ¼ **cup soy sauce**
 ½ **teaspoon sesame oil**

In a small saucepan combine hoisin sauce, soy sauce, and sesame oil. Cook and stir till bubbly. Serve with grilled duck, chicken, beef, or pork. Or, lightly brush sauce on meat during the last 10 minutes of grilling time. Store, covered, in the refrigerator up to 2 weeks. Makes ¾ cup (twelve 1-tablespoon servings.)

Note: The flavors of this sauce are strong and impressive. When serving with grilled meats, use sparingly as you would a steak sauce. When brushing the sauce on meats during grilling, use less of this sauce than you would a typical brush-on barbecue sauce.

Per Serving: 17 calories, 1 g. protein, 3 g. carbohydrate, 0 g. fat, 0 mg. cholesterol, 462 mg. sodium.

SWEET-AND-SOUR SAUCE

 ⅓ **cup chicken broth**
 ¼ **cup packed brown sugar**
 ¼ **cup cider vinegar**
 1 **tablespoon lemon juice**
 1 **tablespoon catsup**
 1 **scallion, minced**
 1½ **teaspoons dry sherry**
 1½ **teaspoons soy sauce**
 1 **tablespoon cornstarch**
 1 **tablespoon cold water**

In a small saucepan combine chicken broth, brown sugar, vinegar, lemon juice, catsup, scallion, sherry, and soy sauce.

Combine cornstarch and cold water. Stir into broth mixture. Cook and stir till thickened and bubbly. Cook and stir 2 minutes more.

Serve warm with grilled pork, chicken, turkey, or fish. Or, brush on meat during the last 10 minutes of grilling time. Makes 1 cup (sixteen 1-tablespoon servings).

Per Serving: 18 calories, 0 g. protein, 4 g. carbohydrate, 0 g. fat, 0 mg. cholesterol, 61 mg. sodium.

FLAVORED BUTTERS

Combine ½ cup of *softened* butter with any number of seasonings to get a quick flavor enhancer for grilled meats, poultry, fish, and vegetables.

Cajun Butter: Add ¼ teaspoon ground red pepper, ⅛ teaspoon black pepper, ⅛ teaspoon garlic powder, and ⅛ teaspoon dried thyme, crushed.

Garlic Butter: Add 2 cloves garlic, minced, or ½ teaspoon garlic powder.

Parmesan Butter: Add 2 tablespoons grated Parmesan cheese and ½ teaspoon dried basil, crushed.

Parsley Butter: Add 1 tablespoon snipped parsley; 1 teaspoon lemon juice; ¼ teaspoon dried savory, crushed; and ⅛ teaspoon salt.

Make your next lamb chop barbecue extra special! Accompany it with refreshing *Yogurt-Cucumber Sauce* (see recipe on page 111).

WEBER TANGY BARBECUE SAUCE

- ½ cup chopped celery
- 3 tablespoons chopped onion
- 2 tablespoons margarine *or* butter
- 1 cup catsup
- ¼ cup lemon juice
- 2 tablespoons sugar
- 2 tablespoons vinegar
- 1 tablespoon Worcestershire sauce
- 1 teaspoon dry mustard
  Dash pepper

In a skillet cook celery and onion in margarine till tender. Add remaining ingredients. Bring to boiling; reduce heat. Cover; simmer 15 minutes. Serve with grilled beef or pork. Makes 1⅔ cups (twenty-six 1-tablespoon servings).

Per Serving: 25 calories, 0 g. protein, 4 g. carbohydrate, 1 g. fat, 0 mg. cholesterol, 128 mg. sodium.

CAJUN SALSA

- ¼ cup finely chopped onion
- ¼ cup finely chopped green pepper
- 2 cloves garlic, minced
- ¼ cup cooking oil
- 1 16-ounce can tomatoes, cut up
- 1 teaspoon sugar
- 1 bay leaf
- ½ teaspoon dried basil, crushed
- ½ teaspoon dried oregano, crushed
- ½ teaspoon black pepper
- ¼ teaspoon ground red pepper
- ¼ to ½ teaspoon bottled hot pepper sauce

Cook onion, green pepper, and garlic in hot oil till tender. Stir in *undrained* tomatoes and remaining ingredients; heat through. Remove bay leaf. Serve with grilled pork or chicken. Makes 2½ cups (forty 1-tablespoon servings).

Note: Pictured on page 108.

Per Serving: 16 calories, 0 g. protein, 1 g. carbohydrate, 1 g. fat, 0 mg. cholesterol, 19 mg. sodium.

SMOKY BARBECUE SAUCE

- ½ cup finely chopped onion
- ½ cup finely chopped green pepper
- ½ cup finely chopped celery
- 2 cloves garlic, minced
- 2 tablespoons cooking oil
- ½ teaspoon dried oregano, crushed
- ½ teaspoon dried basil, crushed
- ½ teaspoon ground cinnamon
- ¼ teaspoon salt
- 2 cups catsup
- 1 cup water
- 3 tablespoons lemon juice *or* cider vinegar
- 4 teaspoons Worcestershire sauce
- 2 teaspoons liquid smoke
  Several dashes bottled hot pepper sauce

In saucepan cook onion, green pepper, celery, and garlic in hot oil over medium heat 5 minutes, stirring frequently. Add oregano, basil, cinnamon, and salt. Cook and stir 2 minutes more.

Stir in catsup, water, lemon juice, Worcestershire sauce, liquid smoke, and hot pepper sauce. Bring to boiling; reduce heat. Simmer, uncovered, 30 minutes, stirring occasionally.

Serve with grilled beef, pork, chicken, fish, or shrimp. Makes 3 cups sauce (forty-eight 1-tablespoon servings).

Per Serving: 19 calories, 0 g. protein, 3 g. carbohydrate, 1 g. fat, 0 mg. cholesterol, 138 mg. sodium.

TERIYAKI MARINADE

  1 **cup soy sauce**
  ½ **cup sake *or* dry vermouth**
  ¼ **cup sugar**
  1 **tablespoon tomato paste (optional)**
  2 **cloves garlic, minced**
  1 **teaspoon grated gingerroot**

Place pork, chicken, or fish in a plastic bag set into a shallow dish. For marinade, combine soy sauce, sake, sugar, tomato paste, garlic, and gingerroot. Pour over meat. Close bag. Marinate in refrigerator 6 hours or overnight, turning bag occasionally. Remove pork, chicken, or fish from marinade and grill according to directions in chart. (See page 16 for pork, page 19 for chicken, or page 20 for fish.) Makes about 1½ cups.

Note: You can cut this marinade in half. Or, prepare the whole recipe and pour desired amount over meat. Refrigerate *unused* portion up to 1 month.

CHUTNEY MARINADE

  1 **8-ounce carton plain yogurt**
  ⅓ **cup chutney, chopped**
  2 **tablespoons cooking oil**
  1 **green onion, sliced**
  2 **teaspoons Dijon-style mustard**
  1½ **teaspoons curry powder**
  1 **teaspoon dried mint leaves, crushed**

Place pork, lamb, or chicken in a plastic bag set into a shallow dish. For marinade, combine yogurt, chutney, oil, green onion, mustard, curry powder, and mint. Pour over meat. Close bag. Marinate in refrigerator 6 hours or overnight, turning bag occasionally. Remove pork, lamb, or chicken from marinade and grill according to directions in chart. (See page 16 for pork, page 17 for lamb, or page 19 for chicken.) Makes about 1 cup.

ORANGE-SOY MARINADE

  ¾ **cup orange juice**
  ¾ **cup soy sauce**
  ¼ **cup dry sherry**
  1 **tablespoon ground ginger**
  4 **cloves garlic, minced**

Place beef, pork, lamb, or chicken in a plastic bag set into a shallow dish. For marinade, in a medium mixing bowl combine orange juice, soy sauce, sherry, ginger, and garlic.

Pour marinade over meat. Close bag. Marinate in refrigerator 6 hours or overnight, turning bag occasionally. Remove beef, pork, lamb, or chicken from marinade and grill according to directions in chart. (See page 15 for beef, page 16 for pork, page 17 for lamb, or page 19 for chicken.) Makes about 1½ cups.

MARINATE LIKE MAGIC

Marinating meat in a plastic bag makes marinating (and cleanup) as easy as 1-2-3. *One,* place the meat in a plastic bag set into a shallow dish. *Two,* pour in the marinade. *Three,* close the bag. You'll find it convenient to redistribute the marinade by simply turning the bag. No stirring or basting needed. And, when marinating is done, just toss the bag.

Here's another way to simplify marinating. Make your marinade out of one ingredient: bottled Italian salad dressing or any other bottled salad dressing with an oil-and-vinegar base.

TANGY BEER MARINADE

1 12-ounce can (1½ cups) beer
2 tablespoons brown sugar
2 tablespoons Worcestershire sauce
1 teaspoon onion salt
1 teaspoon dry mustard

Place beef or pork in a plastic bag set into a shallow dish. For marinade, in a small mixing bowl combine beer, brown sugar, Worcestershire sauce, onion salt, and mustard. Pour over meat. Close bag. Marinate in refrigerator 12 hours or overnight, turning bag occasionally. Remove beef or pork from marinade and grill according to directions in chart. (See page 15 for beef or page 16 for pork.) Makes about 1¾ cups.

Note: If amount of marinade is more than you need, pour desired amount over meat and refrigerate *unused* portion up to 1 month.

TOMATO-SHERRY MARINADE

1 8-ounce can tomato sauce
½ cup dry sherry
¼ cup honey
3 tablespoons brown sugar
3 tablespoons soy sauce
½ teaspoon garlic powder
½ teaspoon ground ginger

Place beef or pork in a plastic bag set into a shallow dish. For marinade, in a small mixing bowl combine tomato sauce, sherry, honey, brown sugar, soy sauce, garlic powder, and ginger. Pour over meat. Close bag. Marinate in refrigerator 6 hours or overnight, turning bag occasionally. Remove beef or pork from bag and grill according to directions in chart. (See page 15 for beef or page 16 for pork.) Makes about 2 cups.

Note: This marinade is especially good with ribs.

KOREAN MARINADE

1 cup soy sauce
⅓ cup cooking oil
¼ cup toasted sesame seed, crushed
2 tablespoons sesame oil
2 tablespoons vinegar
4 cloves garlic, minced
Dash ground red pepper

Place pork, chicken, or fish in a plastic bag set into a shallow dish. For marinade, in a small mixing bowl combine soy sauce, cooking oil, sesame seed, sesame oil, vinegar, garlic, and red pepper. Pour over meat. Close bag. Marinate in refrigerator 6 hours or overnight, turning bag occasionally. Remove pork, chicken, or fish from bag and grill according to directions in chart. (See page 16 for pork, page 19 for chicken, or page 20 for fish.) Makes about 1¼ cups.

Note: Pictured on page 109.

HERB-LEMON MARINADE

½ cup olive *or* cooking oil
½ cup lemon juice
¼ cup white wine Worcestershire sauce
1 tablespoon sugar
2 teaspoons dried basil, crushed
1 teaspoon dried oregano, crushed
3 cloves garlic, minced

Place chicken, turkey, or fish in a plastic bag set into a shallow dish. For marinade, in a small mixing bowl combine olive oil, lemon juice, white wine Worcestershire sauce, sugar, basil, oregano, and garlic. Pour over meat. Close bag. Marinate in refrigerator 6 hours or overnight, turning bag occasionally. Remove chicken, turkey, or fish from bag and grill according to directions in chart. (See page 19 for chicken or turkey or page 20 for fish.) Makes about 1½ cups.

Note: You can refrigerate *unused* marinade up to 1 month. Be sure to discard any marinade that you drain off of the meat.

EXCITING EXTRAS

APPETIZER PIZZAS

Charcoal: Indirect (pages 6-7)
Gas: Indirect/Medium Heat (pages 8-9)

- 1 tablespoon olive oil
- 1 clove garlic, minced
- 1 10-ounce package refrigerated pizza dough
- 1 8-ounce can pizza sauce
- 4 ounces Canadian-style bacon *or* thinly sliced salami, cut into pieces
- ½ cup sliced mushrooms *or* chopped sweet red *or* green pepper
- ¼ cup sliced green onions
- 1 cup shredded mozzarella *or* Monterey Jack cheese (4 ounces)
- ¾ teaspoon dried oregano, crushed

Combine olive oil and garlic; set aside. Cut roll of refrigerated dough into quarters. Flatten *each* quarter into a 5½- to 6-inch circle. Brush both sides of circles with the oil mixture.

Place dough circles in center of the cooking grill. Grill 6 minutes. Transfer circles, grilled side up, to a piece of heavy foil. Spread *each* with some of the pizza sauce. Top with Canadian bacon, mushrooms, and green onions. Sprinkle with cheese and oregano.

Return pizzas on the foil to the cooking grill. Grill 7 to 9 minutes more or till cheese melts and bottoms are light brown. Cut *each* pizza into quarters. Makes 16 servings.

Note: Pictured on page 117.

Per Serving: 93 calories, 5 g. protein, 10 g. carbohydrate, 3 g. fat, 8 mg. cholesterol, 286 mg. sodium.

HAM AND MANGO QUESADILLAS

Charcoal: Direct (pages 6-7)
Gas: Indirect/Medium Heat (pages 8-9)

- 2 tablespoons olive oil
- 1 clove garlic, minced
- 8 7- to 8-inch flour tortillas
- 1½ cups shredded Monterey Jack, Cojack, *or* Chihuahua cheese (6 ounces)
- 4 thin slices fully cooked ham
- 1 medium mango, peeled and thinly sliced, *or* 1 large tomato, thinly sliced
- 2 tablespoons fresh cilantro, chopped
- 1 cup salsa

Combine olive oil and garlic. Brush one side of *four* tortillas with some of the olive oil mixture. Place tortillas, oiled side down, on waxed paper to assemble.

Sprinkle *each* with about ⅓ *cup* of the cheese, spreading cheese to within ¼ inch from edge. Place a slice of ham on top of cheese. Top *each* ham piece with mango slices. Sprinkle lightly with cilantro. Top *each* with remaining tortillas. Brush tops of tortillas with remaining olive oil mixture.

Arrange tortillas on the cooking grill. Grill 30 to 45 seconds per side or till tortillas are lightly browned. Remove from grill and cut *each* into quarters. Serve with salsa. Makes 16 servings.

Per Serving: 132 calories, 6 g. protein, 13 g. carbohydrate, 7 g. fat, 14 mg. cholesterol, 315 mg. sodium.

MUSHROOM AND SCALLOP HORS D'OEUVRES

Charcoal: Direct (pages 6-7)
Gas: Indirect/Medium Heat (pages 8-9)

12 bay scallops
12 medium mushroom caps
 2 tablespoons margarine *or* butter
¼ teaspoon salt
¼ teaspoon lemon-pepper seasoning

Soak 12 wooden toothpicks in water. Gently rinse scallops and mushrooms under cold running water; pat dry. Place a scallop in *each* mushroom cap. Skewer *each* scallop-stuffed mushroom lengthwise with a soaked toothpick. Place in a Weber® 8x5¼-inch aluminum pan. In a small saucepan melt margarine. Stir in salt and lemon-pepper seasoning. Generously brush mixture on the stuffed mushrooms.

Place pan of mushrooms on the cooking grill. Grill 6 to 9 minutes or till mushrooms are tender and scallops are opaque. Makes 12 servings.

Note: The scallop-stuffed mushrooms can also be grilled on four 8-inch skewers. Thread skewers through bottoms of stuffed mushrooms so the scallops inside mushrooms thread onto the skewer, too. Then arrange skewers directly on the cooking grill.

Per Serving: 33 calories, 3 g. protein, 1 g. carbohydrate, 2 g. fat, 5 mg. cholesterol, 105 mg. sodium.

BACON-WRAPPED PINEAPPLE BITES

Charcoal: Direct (pages 6-7)
Gas: Indirect/Medium Heat (pages 8-9)

10 slices bacon
 1 8-ounce can pineapple chunks, drained

Cut bacon slices in half crosswise. In a skillet cook bacon about 4 minutes or till partially cooked. Drain well on paper towels.

Wrap 1 piece of bacon around *each* pineapple chunk. On *each* of four 10-inch skewers, thread bacon-wrapped pineapple through the loose bacon ends to secure. Place skewers on the cooking grill. Grill 5 to 7 minutes or till bacon is crisp and browned. Makes 20 servings.

Per Serving: 25 calories, 1 g. protein, 2 g. carbohydrate, 2 g. fat, 3 mg. cholesterol, 51 mg. sodium.

ROASTED MUSHROOMS

Charcoal: Indirect (pages 6-7)
Gas: Indirect/Medium Heat (pages 8-9)

1 pound fresh mushrooms
2 tablespoons white wine Worcestershire
   sauce
1 tablespoon margarine *or* butter, melted,
   or olive oil
½ teaspoon garlic salt
⅛ teaspoon pepper

Rinse mushrooms; pat dry. Place in center of an 18-inch square of heavy foil. Fold up foil to surround but not enclose mushrooms. Combine Worcestershire sauce, margarine, garlic salt, and pepper; drizzle over mushrooms.

Place open packet in center of the cooking grill. Grill 20 to 30 minutes or till mushrooms are tender. Remove from grill. Spoon juices over mushrooms. Serve mushrooms with a slotted spoon. Makes 8 servings.

Per Serving: 31 calories, 1 g. protein, 4 g. carbohydrate, 2 g. fat, 0 mg. cholesterol, 127 mg. sodium.

Bring the taste of Switzerland to your family and friends with rich-tasting *Raclette-Style Cheese,* melted just right on the grill.

RACLETTE-STYLE CHEESE

Charcoal: Indirect (pages 6-7)
Gas: Indirect/Medium Heat (pages 8-9)

1½ cups shredded process Gruyère *or*
      process Swiss cheese (6 ounces)
  1 cup shredded Gouda cheese (4 ounces)
  1 tablespoon snipped fresh oregano *or*
      basil (*or* 1 teaspoon dried oregano *or*
      basil, crushed)
  2 teaspoons Dijon-style mustard
  1 teaspoon white wine Worcestershire
      sauce
      Several dashes bottled hot pepper sauce
      Pimiento slices (optional)
      Fresh oregano sprigs (optional)
 12 ½-inch-thick slices French bread, toasted

In a small mixing bowl or food processor bowl
combine cheeses; let stand to soften. Add
snipped oregano, mustard, white wine
Worcestershire sauce, and hot pepper sauce.
Beat with an electric mixer on low speed or
cover food processor bowl and process till well
combined. (Mixture will be crumbly.)

Form mixture into a ball. Shape into a 4½-inch
round about 1 inch high. Wrap in clear plastic
wrap and chill several hours or overnight.

Unwrap cheese round; place in a 6-inch cast-iron
skillet. Cut into 6 wedges; separate wedges
slightly. Place skillet in center of the cooking grill.
Grill 6 to 10 minutes or till cheese begins to melt.
(Cheese will continue to melt after it is removed
from the grill.) Top wedges with pimiento slices
and oregano sprigs, if desired. Serve with toasted
French bread. Makes 6 servings.

Note: Toast the bread slices on the grill while
you grill the cheese.

*Per Serving: 288 calories, 17 g. protein, 19 g.
carbohydrate, 16 g. fat, 52 mg. cholesterol,
513 mg. sodium.*

CARAMELIZED ONION AND CHEESE ROUNDS

Charcoal: Indirect (pages 6-7)
Gas: Indirect/Medium Heat (pages 8-9)

  1 large onion, halved lengthwise and
      thinly sliced
  1 tablespoon olive *or* cooking oil
  1 tablespoon margarine *or* butter
 ⅓ cup coarsely chopped walnuts
  1 teaspoon sugar
  1 tablespoon herb mustard *or* Dijon-style
      mustard
  1 tablespoon snipped parsley
 16 ¼-inch-thick slices baguette French
      bread *or* other long, thin, firm bread
 ½ cup shredded mozzarella cheese
      (2 ounces)

In a large skillet cook the sliced onion in oil and
margarine about 3 minutes or just till tender. Add
the chopped walnuts and the sugar. Continue to
cook and stir about 5 minutes or till onion is
slightly caramelized and walnuts are lightly
toasted. Stir in the mustard and parsley.

Place bread slices in a Weber® 13x9-inch
aluminum pan. Spoon onion mixture over *each*
of the bread slices. Sprinkle with the cheese. If
desired, cover bread slices and let stand at room
temperature up to 1 hour.

Place pan in center of the cooking grill. Grill 6 to
8 minutes or just till bottoms are toasted and
onion mixture is heated through. Watch carefully
the last 2 minutes to avoid overbrowning. Makes
8 servings.

*Per Serving: 185 calories, 6 g. protein, 20 g.
carbohydrate, 9 g. fat, 4 mg. cholesterol,
278 mg. sodium.*

CHICKEN WINGS WITH PLUM SAUCE

Charcoal: Indirect (pages 6-7)
Gas: Indirect/Medium Heat (pages 8-9)

    2 pounds chicken wings
    1 10-ounce jar (1 cup) plum preserves
   ¼ cup golden raisins, chopped
    2 tablespoons finely chopped onion
    1 tablespoon white wine vinegar
    2 teaspoons prepared mustard
    2 teaspoons prepared horseradish
    1 clove garlic, minced

Rinse chicken and pat dry. Cut off and discard wing tips. Cut *each* wing at the joint to make 2 sections.

Place the chicken wing pieces in the center of the cooking grill. Grill 30 to 35 minutes or till chicken is tender and the skin is lightly crisp, turning once halfway through grilling time.

Meanwhile, for plum sauce, in a small saucepan combine plum preserves, raisins, onion, wine vinegar, mustard, horseradish, and garlic. Cook and stir till heated through. Serve as a dipping sauce for grilled chicken wing pieces. Makes 6 to 8 servings.

Per Serving: 304 calories, 14 g. protein, 39 g. carbohydrate, 10 g. fat, 44 mg. cholesterol, 73 mg. sodium.

LUAU RIBS

Charcoal: Indirect (pages 6-7)
Gas: Indirect/Medium Heat (pages 8-9)

    3 pounds meaty spareribs *or* pork loin back
       ribs, cut in half crosswise
   ½ cup soy sauce
   ¼ cup packed brown sugar
   ¼ cup water
    2 tablespoons dry sherry
    2 tablespoons unsweetened pineapple juice
   ½ teaspoon grated gingerroot
    1 clove garlic, minced

Cut ribs into 2-rib sections. Place ribs in a plastic bag set into a shallow dish.

For marinade, combine soy sauce, brown sugar, water, sherry, pineapple juice, gingerroot, and garlic. Pour marinade over ribs. Close bag. Marinate in the refrigerator several hours or overnight, turning bag occasionally.

Drain ribs, reserving marinade. Place ribs, meaty side up, in center of the cooking grill. Grill 1 to 1½ hours or till tender, brushing with reserved marinade during the last 15 minutes of grilling time. Makes about 18 servings.

Note: You may be able to find already-cut riblets in the supermarket. If not, have the butcher saw the ribs in half for you.

Per Serving: 137 calories, 9 g. protein, 4 g. carbohydrate, 9 g. fat, 36 mg. cholesterol, 487 mg. sodium.

BACON-CRAB ROLLS

Charcoal: Indirect (pages 6-7)
Gas: Indirect/Medium Heat (pages 8-9)

- 16 slices bacon
- 3 tablespoons soft-style cream cheese
- 1 tablespoon dry sherry
- 1 teaspoon lemon juice
  Few dashes bottled hot pepper sauce
- 1 6-ounce package frozen crabmeat, thawed, drained, flaked, and cartilage removed
- ¾ cup soft bread crumbs (1 slice)
- ¼ cup thinly sliced green onions *or* finely chopped celery

In a skillet cook *half* of the bacon about 4 minutes or just till bacon begins to brown, turning once. Remove. Repeat with remaining bacon. Drain well on paper towels.

In a medium mixing bowl stir together cream cheese, sherry, lemon juice, and hot pepper sauce. Stir in crab, bread crumbs, and green onions. Using about *1 tablespoon* of mixture for *each,* shape into 16 balls. Wrap a bacon slice around *each* ball and secure with wooden toothpick. Arrange in a Weber® 13x9-inch aluminum pan.

Place pan in center of the cooking grill. Grill 13 to 15 minutes or till bacon is crisp and browned and crab filling is hot. Serves 16.

Per Serving: 62 calories, 4 g. protein, 1 g. carbohydrate, 4 g. fat, 16 mg. cholesterol, 151 mg. sodium.

OYSTERS ROCKEFELLER

Charcoal: Direct (pages 6-7)
Gas: Indirect/Medium Heat (pages 8-9)

- Rock salt
- 12 oysters in shells
- 1 teaspoon finely chopped green onion
- 1 small clove garlic, minced
- 2 tablespoons margarine *or* butter
- ⅓ cup fine dry bread crumbs
- 1 tablespoon snipped parsley
- ½ teaspoon dried tarragon, crushed
  Dash pepper

Line a Weber 13x9-inch aluminum pan with rock salt to a depth of about ½ inch. Dampen the salt with some *water.* Place pan on the cooking grill to heat.

Meanwhile, thoroughly wash the oysters. Open shells with an oyster knife or other blunt-tipped knife. Remove oysters and dry. Discard flat top shells and wash deep bottom shells. Place *each* oyster in a bottom shell.

In a small saucepan cook onion and garlic in margarine over medium heat about 1 minute. Remove from heat. Stir in bread crumbs, parsley, tarragon, and pepper. Sprinkle crumb mixture over oysters in shells.

Carefully arrange oyster shells in rock salt. Grill 5 to 8 minutes or till edges of oysters begin to curl and crumbs are lightly toasted. Serves 12.

Note: Pictured on page 116.

Per Serving: 54 calories, 4 g. protein, 4 g. carbohydrate, 2 g. fat, 9 mg. cholesterol, 82 mg. sodium.

SQUASH AND PEPPER KABOBS

Charcoal: Direct (pages 6-7)
Gas: Indirect/Medium Heat (pages 8-9)

- 1 small green pepper, cut into 1-inch pieces
- 1 small sweet red pepper, cut into 1-inch pieces
- 1 small zucchini, sliced ½ inch thick
- 1 small yellow squash, cut into 1-inch pieces
- ½ cup bottled clear Italian salad dressing

Place all vegetables in a plastic bag set into a shallow dish. Pour Italian dressing over vegetables. Close bag. Marinate at room temperature 30 to 60 minutes, turning bag occasionally to distribute marinade.

Drain vegetables, reserving dressing. On four 12-inch skewers alternately thread green pepper, red pepper, zucchini, and yellow squash, leaving space between pieces.

Place kabobs on the cooking grill. Grill 10 to 12 minutes or till vegetables are tender, turning once halfway through grilling time and brushing occasionally with reserved dressing. Serves 4.

Note: To make this light vegetable side dish even lower in calories, use a reduced-calorie Italian salad dressing. Pictured on page 116.

Per Serving: 160 calories, 1 g. protein, 8 g. carbohydrate, 18 g. fat, 0 mg. cholesterol, 147 mg. sodium.

PATIO TOMATOES

Charcoal: Indirect (pages 6-7)
Gas: Indirect/Medium Heat (pages 8-9)

- 6 medium tomatoes
- 6 slices bacon, diced
- ¾ cup chopped onions
- 1½ cups cooked rice
- 1 cup shredded Monterey Jack *or* cheddar cheese (4 ounces)
- 2 tablespoons snipped fresh parsley *or* 2 teaspoons dried parsley flakes
- ¼ teaspoon salt
- ¼ teaspoon dried thyme, crushed
- ⅛ teaspoon pepper·

Cut a thin slice off the stem end of tomatoes. Hollow out tomatoes, leaving a ¼-inch-thick shell. Reserve pulp for another use. Drain tomato shells upside down on paper towels. Set aside.

Meanwhile, in a large skillet cook bacon till crisp. Drain bacon on paper towels, reserving *1 tablespoon* of the bacon drippings in skillet. Add onions to reserved drippings and cook till tender but not brown.

Meanwhile, in a medium mixing bowl combine rice, cheese, parsley, salt, thyme, and pepper. Stir in bacon and onions.

Turn tomato shells right side up. Spoon about *½ cup* of the rice mixture into *each* tomato. Place *each* filled tomato in the center of a 6-inch square of heavy foil. Fold up foil around *each* tomato, leaving top open.

Place tomatoes in foil in center of the cooking grill. Grill about 25 minutes or till heated through. Makes 6 servings.

Note: Pictured on page 116.

Per Serving: 215 calories, 9 g. protein, 20 g. carbohydrate, 12 g. fat, 37 mg. cholesterol, 325 mg. sodium.

LEMON-BUTTERED LEEK AND CAULIFLOWER

Charcoal: Indirect (pages 6-7)
Gas: Indirect/Medium Heat (pages 8-9)

- 1 medium leek
- 2 cups cauliflower flowerets
- 1 tablespoon butter *or* margarine
- 2 teaspoons honey
- ¼ teaspoon salt
- ⅛ teaspoon pepper
- 1 tablespoon lemon juice

Cut green tops from leek to within 2 inches of white portion. Remove 1 or 2 layers of outer skin. Wash, drain, and thinly bias-slice the leek.

Cut an 18x12-inch piece of heavy foil. Place cauliflower and sliced leek in center of foil. Dot with butter. Drizzle with honey and sprinkle with salt and pepper. Bring up 2 opposite edges of foil and, leaving a little space for expansion of steam, tightly seal top, then each end.

Place foil packet in center of the cooking grill. Grill 20 to 25 minutes or till cauliflower and leek are tender.

Just before serving, drizzle with lemon juice and gently stir. Makes 4 servings.

Per Serving: 55 calories, 1 g. protein, 7 g. carbohydrate, 3 g. fat, 8 mg. cholesterol, 166 mg. sodium.

GLAZED CARROTS

Charcoal: Indirect (pages 6-7)
Gas: Indirect/Medium Heat (pages 8-9)

- 6 medium carrots, sliced ¼ inch thick (1 pound)
- 2 tablespoons margarine *or* butter
- ¼ teaspoon finely shredded lemon peel
- 2 tablespoons powdered sugar
- ⅛ teaspoon salt
  Dash pepper

Cut an 18-inch square of heavy foil. Place sliced carrots in center of the foil. Dot with margarine and sprinkle with lemon peel. Bring up 2 opposite edges of foil and, leaving a little space for expansion of steam, tightly seal top, then each end.

Place foil packet in center of the cooking grill. Grill 25 to 30 minutes or till carrots are tender. Remove from grill. Open packet; stir in powdered sugar. Sprinkle with salt and pepper. Serves 4.

Per Serving: 110 calories, 1 g. protein, 14 g. carbohydrate, 6 g. fat, 0 mg. cholesterol, 171 mg. sodium.

GRILLED CORN ON THE COB

Grill fresh ears of corn without taking them out of their husks. Peel the husks back just enough to remove the silk. Return husks to their original position; tie in place with string.

In a sink or large kettle, soak corn in water 30 minutes to prevent husks from burning during grilling. Drain corn. Using the Indirect method (Medium Heat for gas), place the corn in center of the cooking grill. Grill corn in husks 25 to 35 minutes or till tender, turning often. (More mature corn may take 10 to 15 minutes longer.)

Note: If husks are already removed from the corn, omit soaking in water. Wrap each ear in heavy foil and grill as above.

125

Fresh-tasting and
delicately seasoned,
*Summer Vegetable
Potpourri* steams
inside a foil packet
on the grill.

SUMMER VEGETABLE POTPOURRI

Charcoal: Indirect (pages 6-7)
Gas: Indirect/Medium Heat (pages 8-9)

- 8 ounces large whole fresh mushrooms, halved (about 12)
- 2 small yellow summer squash, halved lengthwise and cut into ½-inch-thick slices (2 cups)
- 1 cup pearl onions *or* 1 large onion, cut into chunks
- 1 large stalk celery, bias-sliced into ½-inch pieces (1 cup)
- 2 tablespoons sliced pimiento
- 1 tablespoon white wine Worcestershire sauce
- 1 teaspoon snipped fresh tarragon *or* ¼ teaspoon dried tarragon, crushed
- ½ teaspoon finely shredded lemon peel
- ⅛ teaspoon salt
- 1 tablespoon margarine *or* butter

Cut an 18-inch square of heavy foil. Combine mushrooms, summer squash, onions, celery, and pimiento. Place in center of the foil.

Drizzle vegetables with white wine Worcestershire sauce. Sprinkle with tarragon, lemon peel, and salt. Dot with margarine.

Bring up 2 opposite edges of foil and, leaving a little space for expansion of steam, tightly seal top, then each end.

Place foil packet in center of the cooking grill. Grill 40 to 45 minutes or till vegetables are crisp-tender. Spoon juices over vegetables before serving. Makes 6 servings.

Per Serving: 47 calories, 2 g. protein, 6 g. carbohydrate, 2 g. fat, 0 mg. cholesterol, 103 mg. sodium.

ALABAMA BAKED BEANS

Charcoal: Indirect (pages 6-7)
Gas: Indirect/Medium Heat (pages 8-9)

- 4 slices bacon
- 1 small onion, chopped
- 1 small green pepper, chopped
- 2 16-ounce cans pork and beans with tomato sauce, drained
- ¼ cup packed light brown sugar
- 2 tablespoons vinegar
- 1 tablespoon Worcestershire sauce
- ½ teaspoon dry mustard

In a medium skillet cook bacon till crisp. Drain and crumble, reserving *2 tablespoons* drippings. Cook onion and pepper in reserved drippings till tender. Remove from heat. Stir in beans, sugar, vinegar, Worcestershire sauce, mustard, and bacon pieces; spoon into a Weber® 8x5¼-inch aluminum pan.

Place pan in center of the cooking grill. Grill, uncovered, 30 to 40 minutes or till heated through and of desired consistency, stirring once halfway through grilling time. Serves 4 to 6.

Note: These southern-style beans get their smoky flavor from bacon and their sweet-sour flavor from vinegar and brown sugar. They make a perfect accompaniment to grilled burgers.

Per Serving: 386 calories, 14 g. protein, 60 g. carbohydrate, 13 g. fat, 63 mg. cholesterol, 1,217 mg. sodium.

PILAF PEPPERS

Charcoal: Indirect (pages 6-7)
Gas: Indirect/Medium Heat (pages 8-9)

- 1 cup quick-cooking rice
- 1 cup orange juice
- 1 teaspoon instant chicken bouillon granules
- ¼ cup sliced green onions
- ¼ cup toasted slivered almonds
- 2 teaspoons margarine *or* butter
- 2 large green *or* sweet red peppers

Prepare rice according to package directions, *except* substitute the orange juice for the water and add chicken bouillon granules. Stir green onions, toasted almonds, and margarine into the cooked rice.

Halve peppers lengthwise, removing stem ends, seeds, and membranes.

Spoon *one-fourth* of the rice mixture into *each* of the pepper shell halves. Place stuffed peppers in a Weber® 13x9-inch aluminum pan or in a 13x9x2-inch baking pan. Cover with foil.

Place pan in center of the cooking grill. Grill 20 to 25 minutes or till peppers are crisp-tender and rice mixture is heated through. Serves 4.

Note: If you like your pepper shells very tender, precook the pepper halves 1 minute in a saucepan of boiling water and drain well before filling with the rice mixture.

Per Serving: 196 calories, 4 g. protein, 30 g. carbohydrate, 7 g. fat, 0 mg. cholesterol, 250 mg. sodium.

LEMONY GREEN BEANS

Charcoal: Indirect (pages 6-7)
Gas: Indirect/Medium Heat (pages 8-9)

- 1 9-ounce package frozen cut green beans
- ½ teaspoon sugar
- ¼ teaspoon salt
  Dash pepper
- ½ cup sliced water chestnuts
- ½ small onion, cut into wedges and separated into pieces
- 1 tablespoon margarine *or* butter
- 1 tablespoon lemon juice
  Lemon slices

Partially thaw green beans under hot running water about 30 seconds. Cut an 18x12-inch piece of heavy foil. Place beans in center of foil. Sprinkle with sugar, salt, and pepper. Top with water chestnuts and onion. Dot with margarine.

Bring up long edges of foil and, leaving a little space for expansion of steam, tightly seal top, then each end.

Place foil packet in center of the cooking grill. Grill 20 minutes or till beans are tender. Open packet. Drizzle grilled vegetables with the lemon juice. Serve with lemon slices. Makes 4 servings.

Per Serving: 61 calories, 1 g. protein, 9 g. carbohydrate, 3 g. fat, 0 mg. cholesterol, 177 mg. sodium.

BROCCOLI CASSEROLE

Charcoal: Indirect (pages 6-7)
Gas: Indirect/Medium Heat (pages 8-9)

- 1 small onion, finely chopped (⅓ cup)
- 2 tablespoons margarine *or* butter
- 1 tablespoon flour
- ¼ cup milk
- 1 5-ounce jar American cheese spread
- 1 egg, well beaten
- 1 10-ounce package frozen chopped broccoli, thawed and well drained
- ½ cup soft bread crumbs
- 1 tablespoon margarine *or* butter, melted

In saucepan cook onion in 2 tablespoons margarine till tender but not brown. Stir in flour. Add milk all at once. Cook and stir till thickened and bubbly. Stir in cheese spread. Gradually stir mixture into egg. Add broccoli. Pour into a Weber 8x5¼-inch aluminum pan. Combine bread crumbs and 1 tablespoon margarine; sprinkle over vegetable mixture in pan.

Place in center of the cooking grill. Grill 20 to 25 minutes or till heated through. Serves 4.

Per Serving: 265 calories, 12 g. protein, 13 g. carbohydrate, 19 g. fat, 77 mg. cholesterol, 590 mg. sodium.

ROASTED PEPPERS

Charcoal: Direct (pages 6-7)
Gas: Indirect/Medium Heat (pages 8-9)

- 2 medium sweet red *or* green peppers

Rinse peppers; pat dry. Place whole peppers on the cooking grill. Grill peppers, turning every 5 minutes or till charred evenly on all sides. Remove peppers from grill and place in a paper bag; close tightly. Let stand 10 to 15 minutes. Remove peppers from bag; peel away charred skins. Cut off tops and remove seeds. Serves 2.

Note: Pictured on page 5.

Per Serving: 13 calories, 0 g. protein, 3 g. carbohydrate, 0 g. fat, 0 mg. cholesterol, 2 mg. sodium.

RATATOUILLE

Charcoal: Indirect (pages 6-7)
Gas: Indirect/Medium Heat (pages 8-9)

- 1 small eggplant, cut into ¾-inch cubes (12-ounces)
- 1 small onion, chopped (⅓ cup)
- 1 small zucchini, sliced ½ inch thick
- 1 7½-ounce can tomatoes, cut up
- 1 small green pepper, cut into strips
- ¼ cup olive oil
- 2 cloves garlic, minced
- 1 tablespoon snipped fresh basil *or* 1 teaspoon dried basil, crushed
- ¼ teaspoon salt
- ⅛ teaspoon pepper

Cut two 18x12-inch pieces of heavy foil. Place *half* of the eggplant cubes, onion, zucchini slices, tomatoes, and green pepper in the center of *each* piece of foil.

Fold up foil around vegetables to form a "pan." Combine the olive oil, garlic, basil, salt, and pepper. Drizzle over vegetables. Bring up long edges of foil and, leaving a little space for expansion of steam, tightly seal top, then each end.

Place foil packets in center of the cooking grill. Grill about 35 minutes or till vegetables are very tender. Makes 6 servings.

Per Serving: 112 calories, 2 g. protein, 7 g. carbohydrate, 9 g. fat, 0 mg. cholesterol, 150 mg. sodium.

ROASTED POTATOES

Charcoal: Indirect (pages 6-7)
Gas: Indirect/Medium Heat (pages 8-9)

- 4 medium baking potatoes (6 to 8 ounces each)
- ¼ cup margarine *or* butter, melted
- ¼ teaspoon salt
- ¼ teaspoon pepper

Scrub potatoes thoroughly with a brush. Pat dry. To slice, lay potatoes on their narrow side and slice at ½-inch intervals, slicing *three-fourths* of the way through potato. (To prevent the knife from slicing all the way through potato, place a wooden spoon handle along each side of the potato, if desired.)

Place potatoes, cut side up, in a Weber® 8x5¼-inch aluminum pan. Combine margarine, salt, and pepper. Brush potatoes with some of the margarine mixture. Cover pan with foil.

Place pan in center of the cooking grill. Grill 55 to 60 minutes or till potatoes are tender. Just before serving, brush again with margarine mixture. Makes 4 servings.

Parmesan-Roasted Potatoes: Prepare potatoes as above, *except* omit salt and pepper and stir 2 tablespoons grated *Parmesan cheese* into the melted margarine.

Onion-Roasted Potatoes: Prepare potatoes as above, *except* omit salt and pepper and stir 4 teaspoons dried *minced onion* into the melted margarine.

Italian Roasted Potatoes: Prepare potatoes as above, *except* omit salt and pepper and stir ½ teaspoon dried *basil,* crushed, into the melted margarine.

Tangy Roasted Potatoes: Prepare potatoes as above, *except* omit salt and pepper and stir 1 tablespoon *Dijon-style mustard* into the melted margarine.

Per Serving: 322 calories, 5 g. protein, 51 g. carbohydrate, 12 g. fat, 0 mg. cholesterol, 283 mg. sodium.

HOT GERMAN POTATO SALAD

Charcoal: Indirect (pages 6-7)
Gas: Indirect/Medium Heat (pages 8-9)

- 1 cup water
- ¼ teaspoon salt
- 1 pound potatoes, peeled and cut into ¾-inch cubes
- 6 slices bacon
- 1 cup chopped onions
- ¼ cup sliced celery
- ½ teaspoon caraway seed, crushed
- 2 tablespoons sugar
- 1 tablespoon all-purpose flour
- ¼ cup cider vinegar
- ¼ cup water
- ½ teaspoon brown mustard
- ⅛ teaspoon pepper

In a medium saucepan combine 1 cup water and the salt. Bring to boiling. Add potato cubes. Return to boiling; reduce heat. Simmer, covered, about 10 minutes or till crisp-tender. Drain and set aside.

In a medium skillet cook bacon till crisp. Drain and crumble, reserving *3 tablespoons* drippings. Set bacon aside. Add onions, celery, and caraway seed to reserved drippings. Cook till onions are tender but not brown. Stir in sugar and flour. Add vinegar, ¼ cup water, the mustard, and pepper. Cook and stir till thickened and bubbly.

Remove from heat. Stir in the cooked potatoes and bacon. Cool 10 minutes. Transfer potato salad to a Weber 8x5¼-inch aluminum pan. Cover with foil and refrigerate up to 8 hours.

Place chilled potato salad in covered pan in center of the cooking grill. Grill 35 minutes or till heated through. Makes 4 servings.

Note: This tasty make-ahead salad cuts down on last-minute meal preparations.

Per Serving: 284 calories, 5 g. protein, 32 g. carbohydrate, 16 g. fat, 71 mg. cholesterol, 411 mg. sodium.

TROPICAL SWEET POTATOES

Charcoal: Indirect (pages 6-7)
Gas: Indirect/Medium Heat (pages 8-9)

    3 large sweet potatoes (about 10 to
        12 ounces each)
    3 tablespoons margarine *or* butter
    1 8¼-ounce can crushed pineapple, well
        drained
    ½ teaspoon finely shredded orange peel
    2 tablespoons rum
    1 tablespoon orange juice
    ⅓ cup flaked coconut
    2 tablespoons brown sugar
    2 tablespoons chopped toasted pecans

Scrub potatoes thoroughly with a brush. Pat dry. Prick potatoes with a fork. Bake in a 425° oven about 60 minutes or till tender. [Or, micro-cook on 100% power (high) 15 to 18 minutes or till tender.] Halve potatoes lengthwise. Gently scoop out *each* potato half, leaving a ¼-inch shell. Place pulp in a medium bowl.

With an electric mixer on low speed or a potato masher, beat or mash potato pulp with margarine. Add the pineapple, orange peel, rum, and orange juice. Mix well.

Cut two 20x18-inch squares of heavy foil; place 3 shell halves on *each* piece of foil. Fill *each* shell half with about ⅓ *cup* of the pulp mixture.

For topping, in a small bowl combine coconut, brown sugar, and pecans. Sprinkle about *1 tablespoon* topping over *each* potato half.

For *each* packet, bring up long edges of foil and, leaving a little space for expansion of steam, tightly seal top, then each end.

Place foil packets in center of the cooking grill. Grill 15 to 20 minutes or till potato mixture is heated through. Makes 6 servings.

Note: If desired, substitute 2 tablespoons reserved pineapple juice for the 2 tablespoons rum.

Per Serving: 251 calories, 3 g. protein, 39 g. carbohydrate, 9 g. fat, 0 mg. cholesterol, 82 mg. sodium.

STUFFED BAKED POTATOES

Charcoal: Indirect (pages 6-7)
Gas: Indirect/Medium Heat (pages 8-9)

    3 large baking potatoes (8 ounces each)
    3 tablespoons melted margarine *or* butter
    ½ cup sour cream with chives
    ¼ cup shredded cheddar cheese (1 ounce)

Scrub potatoes; pat dry. Prick potatoes with fork. Micro-cook on 100% power (high) 13 to 16 minutes, rearranging once. Halve potatoes lengthwise. Gently scoop out *each* potato half, leaving thin shell. Beat or mash hot potato pulp with margarine. Mix in sour cream. Mound mixture into shells; place in a Weber 8x5¼-inch aluminum pan. Place pan in center of cooking grill. Grill 30 minutes or till potatoes are heated through. Top *each* with some of the cheese. Grill 2 minutes more or till cheese melts. Serves 6.

Per Serving: 332 calories, 6 g. protein, 40 g. carbohydrate, 17 g. fat, 20 mg. cholesterol, 172 mg. sodium.

GRILLED VEGETABLES

Grill an abundance of fresh vegetables—from asparagus to zucchini—and you can add great variety to your outdoor meals. First, brush the prepared vegetables with cooking oil or a bottled vinaigrette salad dressing. Then place them right on the cooking grill and let them share the heat with the meat. Turn them once, and before long, they'll be crisp-tender and ready to eat.

Asparagus: Wash and scrape off scales. Snap off and discard the woody stems. Arrange spears crosswise on the cooking grill; grill 5 to 7 minutes.

Green onions: Arrange crosswise on cooking grill. Grill about 3 minutes.

Mushrooms: Thread onto skewer. Grill 7 to 9 minutes.

Onion: Cut into ¾-inch slices. Thread slices crosswise onto skewer. Grill 10 to 12 minutes.

Tomatoes: Halve tomatoes crosswise. Grill 5 to 6 minutes. Do not turn.

Zucchini: Halve lengthwise. Grill 7 to 9 minutes.

Pictured clockwise:
Onion-Cheddar Bread, Fennel-Wheat Bread, Salsa Corn Bread, Parmesan-Herb Bread, **and** *Tuna Picnic Bread.*

TUNA PICNIC BREAD

Charcoal: Indirect (pages 6-7)
Gas: Indirect/Medium Heat (pages 8-9)

   1 16-ounce package hot roll mix
   1 cup warm water 120°F (49°C)
   2 tablespoons margarine *or* butter,
        softened
   1 egg
  ¾ cup shredded cheddar *or* Swiss cheese
        (3 ounces)
   1 3¼-ounce can tuna (water pack),
        well drained
  ¼ cup chopped green pepper
  ¼ cup chopped pitted ripe olives
   2 tablespoons fine dry bread crumbs
   1 tablespoon snipped chives
   2 tablespoons milk
   1 beaten egg

Prepare hot roll mix according to package
directions using water, margarine, and egg,
except add ½ *cup* of the shredded cheese just
before kneading. Let dough stand, covered, while
preparing tuna mixture.

Combine tuna, green pepper, olives, bread
crumbs, chives, and remaining cheese. Press
dough into a 12x8-inch rectangle. Brush dough
with milk. Sprinkle tuna mixture over dough to
within 1 inch of edges. Roll up dough tightly,
beginning at short end. Seal seam and ends.
Place dough, seam side down, in a greased
9x5x3-inch loaf pan. Cover; let rise in a warm
place till double (about 45 minutes).

Brush top of loaf with beaten egg. If desired, with
a very sharp knife make 3 cuts about ¼-inch
deep across top of loaf. Place loaf pan in center
of the cooking grill. Grill 35 to 45 minutes or till
bread is golden and tests done. Remove bread
from pan; cool about 1 hour on wire rack. Serve
warm. Refrigerate to store. Makes 16 servings.

Per Serving: 159 calories, 7 g. protein, 22 g.
carbohydrate, 5 g. fat, 35 mg. cholesterol,
294 mg. sodium.

FENNEL-WHEAT BREAD

Charcoal: Indirect (pages 6-7)
Gas: Indirect/Medium Heat (pages 8-9)

   1 16-ounce package hot roll mix
   1 cup whole wheat flour
  1½ teaspoons fennel seed *or* dillseed,
        crushed
  1⅓ cups warm water 120°F (49°C)
   2 tablespoons margarine *or* butter,
        softened
   1 egg
  ½ cup shredded Swiss cheese (2 ounces)
   1 beaten egg
   1 tablespoon water
        Fennel seed *or* dillseed

In a large bowl combine flour mixture and packet
of yeast from hot roll mix. Stir in whole wheat
flour and 1½ teaspoons fennel seed. Stir in
the warm water, the margarine, and egg till
mixture forms soft dough. Knead dough with the
cheese on a lightly floured surface till cheese is
mixed into the dough (about 5 minutes).

Shape dough into a round; place in a greased
8x8x2-inch baking pan. Cover; let rise in a warm
place till double (about 45 minutes).

Combine beaten egg and 1 tablespoon water;
brush over the top of the loaf. Sprinkle with
fennel seed. With a very sharp knife, make 3 or
4 diagonal cuts about ¼ inch deep across the
top of the loaf.

Place pan in center of the cooking grill. Grill
30 to 35 minutes or till bread is golden and tests
done. Remove bread from pan; cool on wire
rack. Makes 12 servings.

Per Serving: 216 calories, 8 g. protein, 35 g.
carbohydrate, 5 g. fat, 40 mg. cholesterol,
306 mg. sodium.

GOLDEN FRUIT LOAF

Charcoal: Indirect (pages 6-7)
Gas: Indirect/Medium Heat (pages 8-9)

    1   16-ounce package hot roll mix
    1   cup warm water 120°F (49°C)
    2   tablespoons margarine *or* butter,
           softened
    1   egg
    ⅓   cup packed brown sugar
    1   teaspoon ground cinnamon
    ¼   teaspoon ground nutmeg
    1   tablespoon margarine *or* butter, melted
    ½   of a 6-ounce package (⅔ cup) dried
           fruit bits
    1   beaten egg
    1   tablespoon water

Prepare hot roll mix according to package directions, using the warm water, the 2 tablespoons margarine, and egg. Cover; let rest 5 minutes.

Press dough into a 12x8-inch rectangle. Combine brown sugar, cinnamon, and nutmeg. Brush dough with the 1 tablespoon melted margarine; sprinkle with brown sugar mixture. Sprinkle with the dried fruit bits. Roll up dough tightly, beginning at short end. Seal seam and ends. Place dough, seam side down, in a greased 9x5x3-inch loaf pan. Cover; let rise in a warm place till double (about 45 minutes).

Combine beaten egg and the 1 tablespoon water; brush over top of loaf. Place loaf pan in center of the cooking grill. Grill about 40 minutes or till bread is golden and tests done. Remove bread from pan; cool on a wire rack. Serve at room temperature. Makes 16 servings.

Per Serving: 159 calories, 4 g. protein, 30 g. carbohydrate, 3 g. fat, 20 mg. cholesterol, 232 mg. sodium.

ONION-CHEDDAR BREAD

Charcoal: Indirect (pages 6-7)
Gas: Indirect/Medium Heat (pages 8-9)

    1   16-ounce package hot roll mix
    1   cup warm water 120°F (49°C)
    1   cup shredded cheddar cheese (4 ounces)
    2   large onions, sliced and separated
           into rings (2 cups)
    2   green onions, sliced
    1   clove garlic, minced
    2   tablespoons margarine *or* butter
    ¼   teaspoon dried basil, crushed
    ¼   teaspoon dried tarragon, crushed

Prepare hot roll mix according to package directions, using the warm water and omitting butter and egg. On a lightly floured surface knead dough with ¾ *cup* of the cheese till cheese is mixed into the dough (about 5 minutes). Cover and let rest while preparing onions.

In a medium skillet cook onions and garlic in margarine over medium-high heat till onions are tender; reduce heat to medium and cook till onions are lightly browned. Stir in basil and tarragon; cook 1 to 3 minutes more.

Press dough evenly into a greased 9-inch round aluminum foil or metal baking pan. Sprinkle remaining cheese over dough; spoon onion mixture over cheese. Cover and let rise in a warm place till double (45 to 60 minutes).

Using the handle of a wooden spoon, make indentations in the dough at 2-inch intervals. Place pan in center of the cooking grill. Grill 30 to 40 minutes or till bread is golden brown. Makes 6 to 8 servings.

Note: Pictured on page 132.

Per Serving: 393 calories, 13 g. protein, 60 g. carbohydrate, 12 g. fat, 20 mg. cholesterol, 684 mg. sodium.

SALSA CORN BREAD

Charcoal: Indirect (pages 6-7)
Gas: Indirect/Medium Heat (pages 8-9)

  1 **beaten egg**
  1 **8½-ounce package corn muffin mix**
  ¼ **cup water**
  ¼ **cup hot *or* mild salsa**
  2 **tablespoons canned chopped green
       chili peppers**

In a mixing bowl combine egg, corn muffin mix,
water, salsa, and green chilies; stir just till
moistened. Pour batter into a greased 8x8x2-inch
baking pan or 9x5x3-inch loaf pan. Place pan in
center of the cooking grill. Grill 25 to 30 minutes
or till a toothpick inserted near the center comes
out clean. Serve warm. Makes 8 servings.

Note: Pictured on page 132.

*Per Serving: 138 calories, 3 g. protein, 23 g.
carbohydrate, 4 g. fat, 27 mg. cholesterol,
283 mg. sodium.*

PARMESAN-HERB BREAD

Charcoal: Indirect (pages 6-7)
Gas: Indirect/Medium Heat (pages 8-9)

  1 **loaf unsliced Italian *or* Vienna bread**
  ½ **cup margarine *or* butter, melted**
  1 **clove garlic, minced**
  1 **teaspoon dried basil, crushed**
  ½ **teaspoon dried oregano, crushed**
  ¼ **teaspoon dried sage, crushed**
  ¼ **cup grated Parmesan cheese**

Cut bread into ¾-inch slices, cutting to but not
through bottom of loaf. Combine margarine,
garlic, basil, oregano, and sage; brush on bread
slices and on top of loaf. Sprinkle bread slices
and top of loaf with cheese. Wrap in heavy foil.
Place in center of cooking grill. Grill 15 to 20
minutes or till heated through. Serves 12 to 16.

Note: Pictured on page 132.

*Per Serving: 177 calories, 4 g. protein, 22 g.
carbohydrate, 8 g. fat, 1 mg. cholesterol,
327 mg. sodium.*

GRILLED FRENCH BREAD

Charcoal: Indirect (pages 6-7)
Gas: Indirect/Medium Heat (pages 8-9)

  1 **16-ounce loaf French *or* Italian bread**
  ½ **cup margarine *or* butter, softened**

Cut bread crosswise into 1-inch slices, cutting to
but not through bottom crust. Spread cut surfaces
with softened margarine. Wrap loaf in heavy foil;
seal with double fold on top and ends. Place
bread in center of the cooking grill. Grill 15 to
20 minutes or till heated through. Makes 15 or
16 servings.

Caraway-Cheese Bread: Prepare as above,
except stir 1 cup shredded process *American
cheese* (4 ounces), ½ cup *mayonnaise* or *salad
dressing*, and 1 to 2 teaspoons *caraway seed* into
the softened margarine before spreading on the
cut surfaces of bread.

Parmesan-Chive Bread: Prepare as above,
except stir ¼ cup grated *Parmesan cheese* and
2 tablespoons snipped *chives or* finely chopped
green onion into the softened margarine before
spreading on the cut surfaces of bread.

Blue Cheese-Herb Bread: Prepare as above,
except stir 1 cup crumbled *blue cheese*
(4 ounces); 1 tablespoon snipped *parsley;*
2 teaspoons dried *minced onion;* 1 teaspoon
dried *rosemary,* crushed; and 1 teaspoon dried
basil, crushed, into the softened margarine before
spreading on the cut surfaces of bread.

Garlic-Herb Bread: Prepare as above, *except* stir
1 tablespoon finely snipped *parsley;* 1 or 2 cloves
garlic, minced; ¼ teaspoon dried *basil,* crushed;
¼ teaspoon dried *oregano,* crushed; and dash
pepper into the softened margarine before
spreading on the cut surfaces of bread.

*Per Serving: 141 calories, 3 g. protein, 15 g.
carbohydrate, 7 g. fat, 0 mg. cholesterol,
247 mg. sodium.*

CARAMEL-SAUCED FRUIT KABOBS

Charcoal: Direct (pages 6-7)
Gas: Indirect/Medium Heat (pages 8-9)

  1 **8-ounce container soft-style cream
      cheese (plain *or* with pineapple)**
 ½ **cup caramel ice-cream topping**
 ½ **cup chopped toasted pecans**
  1 **to 2 tablespoons milk (optional)**
  2 **large bananas**
  2 **cups fresh *or* canned pineapple chunks**
  1 **large apple, cored and cut into
      1½-inch chunks**

For caramel sauce, in a small saucepan combine
cream cheese and caramel ice-cream topping.
Cook and stir till cream cheese melts. Stir in
pecans. If desired, add milk to make a sauce of
thinner consistency.

Meanwhile, bias-slice bananas into 1½-inch
chunks. On 6 skewers alternately thread
pineapple chunks, apple chunks, and banana
chunks, threading banana pieces crosswise so
skewers pierce sides, not center, of banana.

Place kabobs on the cooking grill. Grill about
6 minutes or till heated through, turning once.
Brush with caramel sauce and grill 1 minute
more. Pass remaining sauce. Makes 4 servings.

Note: You can also grill the fruit kabobs Indirect
on charcoal. Grill them 8 minutes, then brush
with sauce and grill 1 minute more.

*Per Serving: 513 calories, 7 g. protein, 59 g.
carbohydrate, 30 g. fat, 60 mg. cholesterol,
304 mg. sodium.*

RUM PINEAPPLE BOATS

Charcoal: Indirect (pages 6-7)
Gas: Indirect/Medium Heat (pages 8-9)

  1 **pineapple**
 ⅓ **cup margarine *or* butter**
 ¼ **cup packed brown sugar**
  3 **tablespoons rum**
 ½ **teaspoon ground cinnamon**
 ⅛ **teaspoon ground cloves**
 ⅛ **teaspoon ground nutmeg**

Use a sharp knife to quarter the fresh pineapple
lengthwise. (Do not remove crown.) Remove
hard core from pineapple quarters. Loosen
pineapple flesh from shell. Cut the flesh of *each*
quarter into ½-inch-thick slices.

In a small saucepan melt margarine. Stir in brown
sugar, rum, cinnamon, and cloves.

Wrap pineapple crowns in heavy foil to prevent
burning. Place pineapple quarters, shell side
down, in center of the cooking grill. Grill about
15 minutes or till pineapple is heated through,
basting every 5 minutes with the rum mixture.

Just before serving, remove foil from crowns.
Sprinkle *each* serving with nutmeg. Serves 4.

Note: Pictured on page 117.

*Per Serving: 289 calories, 1 g. protein, 33 g.
carbohydrate, 16 g. fat, 0 mg. cholesterol,
185 mg. sodium.*

APPLE CRISP

Charcoal: Indirect (pages 6-7)
Gas: Indirect/Medium Heat (pages 8-9)

  5 **cups sliced, peeled apples**
  ¾ **cup packed brown sugar**
  ¾ **cup quick-cooking rolled oats**
  ½ **cup all-purpose flour**
  ½ **teaspoon ground cinnamon**
  ½ **teaspoon ground nutmeg**
  ½ **cup margarine *or* butter**
     Whipped cream *or* vanilla ice cream
     (optional)

Place apple slices in an 8x8-inch foil pan or an 8x8x2-inch metal baking pan. Stir in ¼ *cup* of the brown sugar.

For topping, in a medium mixing bowl combine remaining brown sugar, oats, flour, cinnamon, and nutmeg. Cut in margarine till mixture resembles coarse crumbs.

Sprinkle topping over apples. Place pan in center of the cooking grill. Grill 30 to 35 minutes or till apples are tender and topping is crisp. Serve warm with whipped cream, if desired. Serves 6.

Note: Use either cooking apples (such as jonathan, winesap, and granny smith) or eating apples (such as golden delicious) in this recipe.

Per Serving: 371 calories, 3 g. protein, 55 g. carbohydrate, 16 g. fat, 0 mg. cholesterol, 192 mg. sodium.

HONEY-LIME BANANAS

Charcoal: Indirect (pages 6-7)
Gas: Indirect/Medium Heat (pages 8-9)

  4 **bananas**
  4 **teaspoons honey**
  1 **lime, cut into 8 wedges**

Without removing banana peel, slice bananas in half lengthwise. Place bananas, peel side down, in center of the cooking grill. Grill 6 to 8 minutes or till heated through.

Arrange bananas on serving plates; drizzle with honey. Squeeze lime wedges over bananas. Makes 4 servings.

Per Serving: 131 calories, 1 g. protein, 34 g. carbohydrate, 1 g. fat, 0 mg. cholesterol, 2 mg. sodium.

LAST COURSE? OF COURSE!

It makes all the sense in the world to prepare dessert on your Weber® grill. After all, the grill is still hot from the main course. Why not let the grill cook dessert for you while you are enjoying the entrée?

Want another excuse for grilling dessert? You can enjoy warm cakes, cobblers, and other fabulous fruit desserts without heating up the kitchen. In the heat of summer, that is a real advantage!

Buttery rich *Sherry-Sauced Pears* accompanied by vanilla ice cream—it's the all-out way to end your grill out!

SHERRY-SAUCED PEARS

Charcoal: Indirect (pages 6-7)
Gas: Indirect/Medium Heat (pages 8-9)

- 3 medium pears
- ⅓ cup packed brown sugar
- ¼ cup water
- ¼ cup cream sherry *or* port
- 1 tablespoon margarine *or* butter
- 1 tablespoon lemon juice
- ½ teaspoon ground cinnamon
- ⅓ cup chopped toasted pecans
- 1½ cups vanilla ice cream

Halve pears lengthwise. Peel pears. Remove and discard cores. Place halves, cut side down, on cutting board. To fan each pear half, make lengthwise cuts from blossom end to, but not through, stem end.

Cut six 18x12-inch pieces of heavy foil. Place *one* pear half, cut side down, on *one* piece of foil. Repeat with remaining pear halves and foil. Fold up foil around pears.

In a small saucepan combine brown sugar, water, sherry, margarine, lemon juice, and cinnamon. Cook and stir over medium heat till heated through. Immediately spoon about *2 tablespoons* of the mixture over *each* pear half.

Bring up long edges of foil and, leaving a little space for expansion of steam, tightly seal top, then each end. Place foil packets in center of the cooking grill. Grill about 15 minutes or till pears are tender.

Remove pears from grill; open packets. Carefully transfer pears to dessert dishes, spooning sauce over top. Sprinkle *each* serving with about *1 tablespoon* of the pecans. Serve with ice cream. Makes 6 servings.

Per Serving: 237 calories, 2 g. protein, 35 g. carbohydrate, 10 g. fat, 15 mg. cholesterol, 58 mg. sodium.

GRILLED FRUIT MEDLEY

Charcoal: Indirect (pages 6-7)
Gas: Indirect/Medium Heat (pages 8-9)

- 2 medium bananas, cut into chunks
- 2 medium plums, pitted and cut into wedges
- 2 medium peaches *or* nectarines, peeled, pitted, and cut into wedges
- ¼ cup strawberry jelly
- 2 tablespoons margarine *or* butter, melted
- 2 tablespoons orange liqueur
- 2 tablespoons toasted slivered almonds

On four 18x12-inch pieces of heavy foil, evenly divide the bananas, plums, and peaches. Stir together jelly, margarine, and liqueur. Spoon some over *each* packet of fruit.

For *each* packet, bring up the long edges of foil and, leaving a little space for expansion of steam, tightly seal top, then each end.

Place foil packets in center of the cooking grill. Grill 8 to 10 minutes or till fruit is heated through. Remove from grill. Open packets. Sprinkle *each* with about *2 teaspoons* of the almonds. Serves 4.

Note: Serve this delightful fruit combination all by itself or over slices of angel food cake or pound cake.

Per Serving: 245 calories, 2 g. protein, 40 g. carbohydrate, 8 g. fat, 0 mg. cholesterol, 73 mg. sodium.

RASPBERRY COBBLER

Charcoal: Indirect (pages 6-7)
Gas: Indirect/Medium Heat (pages 8-9)

  3 cups fresh *or* frozen raspberries *or*
      blueberries
  ⅓ cup granulated sugar
1½ teaspoons cornstarch
  ¾ cup packaged biscuit mix
  ¼ cup chopped walnuts
  2 tablespoons brown sugar
  ¼ teaspoon ground cinnamon
  3 tablespoons milk *or* light cream
  1 cup vanilla ice cream

Thaw berries, if frozen; do not drain. In a medium saucepan combine berries, the ⅓ cup sugar, and the cornstarch. Cook and stir over medium heat till thickened and bubbly. Keep hot.

For topping, in a small mixing bowl combine the biscuit mix, walnuts, brown sugar, and cinnamon. Stir in milk till moistened. Transfer hot fruit to a Weber® 8x5¼-inch aluminum pan or an 8x1½-inch round baking pan. Drop topping into 4 mounds onto hot berry filling.

Place pan in center of the cooking grill. Grill 20 to 25 minutes or till topping is lightly golden brown and a toothpick inserted into topping comes out clean. Serve warm with vanilla ice cream. Makes 4 servings.

Per Serving: 349 calories, 5 g. protein, 59 g. carbohydrate, 12 g. fat, 16 mg. cholesterol, 301 mg. sodium.

FRUIT AND HONEY APPLE SLICES

Charcoal: Indirect (pages 6-7)
Gas: Indirect/Medium Heat (pages 8-9)

  ⅓ cup chopped mixed dried fruit, raisins,
      or mixed dried fruit bits
  ¼ teaspoon finely shredded orange peel
  3 tablespoons coconut
  2 tablespoons honey
  ¼ teaspoon ground cinnamon
  2 medium baking apples
  2 tablespoons orange juice
  1 tablespoon margarine *or* butter

In a mixing bowl combine dried fruit and orange peel. Stir in coconut, honey, and cinnamon. Core the apples; slice *each* of the apples into 8 rings.

Cut two 18x12-inch pieces of heavy foil. Place *half* of the apple slices in the center of 1 piece of foil. Sprinkle with *half* of the dried fruit mixture and *1 tablespoon* of orange juice. Repeat with the second piece of foil and the remaining apple slices, dried fruit mixture, and orange juice. Dot fruit with margarine.

For *each* packet, bring up the long edges of foil and, leaving a little space for expansion of steam, tightly seal top, then each end. Place foil packets in center of the cooking grill. Grill 15 to 20 minutes or till apple slices are tender. Serves 2.

Note: If you like, serve these naturally sweetened apple slices with creamy vanilla yogurt.

Per Serving: 301 calories, 2 g. protein, 61 g. carbohydrate, 9 g. fat, 0 mg. cholesterol, 87 mg. sodium.

PEACHES 'N' CREAM

Charcoal: Indirect (pages 6-7)
Gas: Indirect/Medium Heat (pages 8-9)

- ⅓ **cup soft-style cream cheese**
- 2 **tablespoons sugar**
- 2 **tablespoons raisins (optional)**
  Dash ground nutmeg
- 2 **large peaches** *or* **nectarines**
- 1 **tablespoon chopped pecans**

In a small mixing bowl combine cream cheese, sugar, raisins (if desired), and nutmeg. Set aside.

Cut peaches in half lengthwise. Remove and discard pits. Cut a thin slice from the bottom of *each* half so the fruit sits level.

Cut four 15x12-inch pieces of heavy foil. Place *one* of the peach halves on *each* piece of foil. Spoon *one-fourth* of the cream cheese mixture into the center of *each* peach half. Bring edges of each piece of foil together; seal loosely.

Place bundles, seam side up, in center of the cooking grill. Grill about 10 minutes or till fruit is tender. Open bundles and sprinkle with pecans. Makes 4 servings.

Note: During grilling, the sweetened cream cheese melts to form a luscious sauce over the warm fruit.

Per Serving: 137 calories, 2 g. protein, 16 g. carbohydrate, 8 g. fat, 20 mg. cholesterol, 67 mg. sodium.

ROCKY ROAD CAKE

Charcoal: Indirect (pages 6-7)
Gas: Indirect/Medium Heat (pages 8-9)

- ¾ **cup all-purpose flour**
- 2 **tablespoons unsweetened cocoa powder**
- ¼ **teaspoon baking soda**
  Dash salt
- ⅓ **cup margarine** *or* **butter**
- ¾ **cup sugar**
- 1 **egg**
- ¼ **cup water**
- ¼ **cup buttermilk**
- ½ **teaspoon vanilla**
- ½ **cup semisweet chocolate pieces**
- ½ **cup tiny marshmallows**
- ¼ **cup chopped toasted nuts**

In a small mixing bowl combine flour, cocoa powder, baking soda, and salt. In a medium saucepan melt margarine; remove from heat. Stir in sugar. Add egg; stir till well blended. Add water, buttermilk, and vanilla; mix well. Gradually add flour mixture, beating just till combined. (Batter will be thin.)

Pour into a well-greased Weber 8x5¼-inch aluminum pan. Place pan in center of the cooking grill. Grill about 25 minutes or till a toothpick inserted near center comes out clean.

Place cake on a wire rack. Immediately sprinkle with chocolate pieces. Let stand 2 minutes. Gently spread chocolate pieces over cake and sprinkle with marshmallows and nuts. Serve warm or at room temperature. Makes 6 to 8 servings.

Per Serving: 384 calories, 5 g. protein, 51 g. carbohydrate, 20 g. fat, 36 mg. cholesterol, 202 mg. sodium.

INDEX

143